BETTER HOMES AND GARDENS®

creative

crockery

cooking

Meredith® Books
Des Moines, Iowa

Meredith Books
1716 Locust Street
Des Moines, Iowa 50309-3023
www.meredithbooks.com

First Edition. Printed in the United States of America
ISBN: 0-696-23448-3
Excerpted from Great Recipes Collection: Crockery Dinners

introduction

More than 180 slow cooker recipes for everything from appetizers to main meals give you variety, value—and guaranteed great taste.

There's nothing quite like walking in the door after a busy day away from home to the mouthwatering aroma and eager anticipation of a dinner that's ready and waiting. Your slow cooker lets you do just that. Crockery Cooking gives you a generous helping of opportunities to put that most humble and handy appliance to good use.

Creative Crockery Cooking is chock-full of failproof recipes that will please everyone in your family. In the mood for comfort food? Try Chicken and Dumplings or Old-Fashioned Beef Stew. Need something to munch on while you watch the Sunday game? Toss Buffalo Wings in the slow cooker in the morning and serve them with Blue Cheese Dip (and lots of napkins) at kick-off. Need something just a little bit special for dinner guests? Look no further than Winter Night Osso Buco or Mustard-Sauced Lamb and Artichokes. In addition to the more than 180 family-pleasing recipes for appetizers, soups and stews, meats, poultry, and vegetables, a special section called Slow Cooking 101 (see page 6) gives you everything you need to know about using your slow cooker safely and getting the best results. It also provides a few culinary tricks, such as how to make a spice bag for mulled beverages and how to fashion aluminum foil handles for lifting meat loaves out of the slow cooker with ease.

Using your slow cooker has always been easy and convenient. With Creative Crockery Cooking, it is now a lot more interesting and fun.

Kielbasa Stew, page 85

contents

slow cooking 101

Dinner that cooks by itself while you're at the office, at play, or working around the house is a dream come true to busy families who, despite their schedules, want to enjoy a delicious home-cooked meal together at the end of a long day.

The make-it-and-forget-it nature of crockery cooking is the main reason for the humble appliance's popularity—not to mention that it makes more economical cuts of meat butter-knife tender and fills the house with wonderful aromas as dinner simmers undisturbed. Before you rush into slow cooking, however, there are a few simple things you might need to know—starting with the types of slow cookers that are available.

Slow Cooker Models

The most common type of slow cooker is the continuous slow cooker. All of the recipes in this book were tested in this type of cooker, which continuously cooks foods slowly at a very low wattage. The heating coils or elements are wrapped around the sides of the cooker and stay on continuously. This type of cooker generally has fixed settings: low, which is about 200°F; high, which is about 300°F; and, in some models, automatic (these shift from high to low heat automatically). The ceramic liner may or may not be removable.

The other type of cooker—the intermittent cooker—is not recommended for the recipes in this cookbook. In intermittent cookers, the heating elements or coils are located below the food container and cycle on and off during operation. If your cooker has a dial indicating temperatures in degrees, this is the type of cooker you have. Because the recipes in this book need continuous slow temperatures, this cooker will not cook the food properly.

Slow cookers come in a range of sizes, but the most widely available—and most useful— have a capacity of 3½, 4, 5, or 6 quarts. The recipes in this book recommend the size to use. Check the capacity of your cooker to see whether it fits the recommendation in the recipe. For best results the slow cooker must be at least half full and no more than two-thirds full. If your budget and storage space can afford it, it doesn't hurt to have two slow cookers—a smaller and a larger one—to be able to make nearly any recipe. Slow cookers also can be either round, which is perfect for soups and stews, or oval, which more easily accommodates roasts and cut-up whole chickens. A basic but good quality 3½-quart model of either shape can be found for less than $30, and the larger models for about $50.

Cooking Times

If you want dinner to cook all day, use the low-heat setting of your cooker, and the corresponding recommended time for low heat. For a shorter cooking time, use the high-heat setting. Cooking times may vary depending on the cooker, but the recommended timings generally will work with all continuous slow cookers. When a recipe recommends only one cooking setting and time, do not use the other setting because your recipe may not turn out properly.

As good as something may smell, resist the temptation to lift the lid during cooking. Removing the lid—even for a moment—allows significant amounts of heat to escape and extends the cooking time. Because the slow cooker cooks at such low temperatures, it is unable to quickly recover the lost heat and return to the desired temperature. An uncovered cooker can lose up to 20 degrees of cooking heat in as little as 2 minutes. A quick peek will change the temperature by only 1 or 2 degrees. When a recipe calls for lifting the lid near the end of the cooking time, do so as quickly as possible, replacing the lid as soon as you can.

Safety First

Foods prepared in a slow cooker are safe to eat even though they cook at low temperatures. The long cooking time and the steam that forms in the tightly covered container destroy bacteria. To ensure that your food is safe to eat, though, take a few precautions. Clean the cooker and all utensils before you start. Always completely thaw raw meat or poultry before adding it to the cooker. Do not use the slow cooker for very large pieces of meat. Cut in half any roasts that are larger than 2½ pounds.

Many cooks buy large-capacity slow cookers so they can cook once and have enough leftovers for another meal. Be sure to remove cooked food from the crockery cooker before storing it. If you store the warm food and the crockery liner in the refrigerator, the food may not cool down quickly enough. Cooling foods quickly is the key to keeping them safe from bacteria. Store leftovers in a storage container and refrigerate or freeze.

Time-Savers

If you need to leave early in the morning—or if your morning will be very busy—you can start your preparations the previous night. Place cleaned and chopped vegetables, seasonings, and liquids into a bowl or in the slow cooker liner if it is removable. Do not mix raw meat or poultry with other raw ingredients. Chill the vegetables. The following morning, assemble all of the ingredients in the cooker (in the order recommended in the recipe), cover, and spend the rest of the day as you like.

There may be times when you will be gone a bit longer than the recipe needs to cook. In these instances, you can use an automatic timer to start your cooker (some slow cooker models have timers on them already). These can be purchased at a hardware store.

When using the timer, prepare the recipe and thoroughly chill all of the ingredients. When you're ready to leave the house, fill the cooker, plug it into the timer, set the timer, and turn on the cooker. It's very important to remember that food should never stand more than two hours before it begins cooking. Also, do not use this method for recipes that include frozen fish.

Slow Cooking with Dairy Products

Milk, cream, and natural cheeses break down from long cooking times. Use substitutes such as reconstituted condensed soups and nonfat dry milk powder. You can also use evaporated milk, if you add it during the last 30 to 60 minutes of cooking time. Natural cheeses can be stirred into a finished dish just before serving.

Tricks of the Trade

There are a couple of techniques commonly used in slow cooking that are helpful to know how to do. Many hot beverages such as spiced cider and mulled wine call for using a spice bag. To make a spice bag, cut a double thickness of 100-percent-cotton cheesecloth in a 6-inch square. Place spices in the center of the square. Bring up the corners of the cheesecloth and tie with clean 100-percent-cotton string.

Foil handles make it easy to lift a soufflé dish or meat loaf out of the slow cooker. To make foil handles, tear off three 18×2-inch strips of heavy foil or use regular foil folded to double thickness. Crisscross the foil strips in a spoke design. (Place them on a large sheet of waxed paper if shaping meat loaf.) Place the soufflé dish or shaped meat loaf in the center of the spoke before cooking.

Slow Cooker Care

To keep your slow cooker in good condition and ensure that it will be around to make many satisfying meals for years to come, follow a few simple guidelines.

First, never put cold food or water into a hot cooker, or a hot cooker in the refrigerator. Sudden temperature changes can crack the ceramic liner. Also, never immerse the cooker or the cord in water—and always unplug the cooker before cleaning it.

To clean the slow cooker, wipe the liner with a soft cloth and hot soapy water only. Avoid using abrasive cleaners and cleansing pads. Removable ceramic liners can be washed in the dishwasher or by hand.

appetizers

Get the party started—and keep it going—with these tasty snacks.
Everything from creamy dips to Buffalo wings
will keep your guests happy—and you enjoying their company.

Buffalo Wings with Blue Cheese Dip, page 27

Almost-A-Meal Queso

The dried, smoked jalapeños called chipotle peppers have a spicy, almost chocolatey flavor. They give this hearty dip lots of zip. Look for them in the produce section of your supermarket.

Prep: 20 minutes **Cook:** 1 to 2 hours on high **Makes:** 8 cups (sixty four, 2-tablespoon servings)

1 pound ground beef

1 large onion, chopped

2 cloves garlic, minced

2 pounds American cheese, cubed

½ of a 16-ounce link cooked kielbasa or smoked sausage, quartered lengthwise and sliced

1 14½-ounce can diced tomatoes, undrained

1 4-ounce can chopped green chiles, undrained

2 to 3 chipotle peppers in adobo sauce, drained and chopped (optional)

1 tablespoon chili powder

1½ teaspoons Worcestershire sauce

½ teaspoon ground black pepper

Tortilla chips

1. In a large skillet cook the ground beef, onion, and garlic until beef is no longer pink; drain. Add to a 3½- or 4-quart slow cooker. Stir in cheese, sausage, tomatoes, green chiles, chipotle peppers (if desired), chili powder, Worcestershire sauce, and black pepper.

2. Cover; cook on high-heat setting for 1 to 2 hours until cheese melts, stirring after 1 hour. To serve, keep warm on low-heat setting, stirring occasionally. Serve with tortilla chips.

Nutrition Facts per serving: 82 calories, 6 g total fat, 20 mg cholesterol, 258 mg sodium, 1 g carbohydrate, 5 g protein.

Supreme Pizza Fondue

For a truly supreme version of this savory fondue, use a combination of sausage, pepperoni, Canadian bacon, and 1/2 teaspoon each of basil and oregano.

Prep: 20 minutes **Cook:** 3 hours on low **Makes:** 5½ cups (ten, ½-cup servings)

---

1. In a large skillet cook the sausage, onion, and garlic until meat is brown. Drain off fat.

2. In a 3½- or 4-quart slow cooker combine spaghetti sauce, mushrooms, pepperoni and basil. Stir in the meat mixture.

3. Cover; cook on low-heat setting for 3 hours. If desired, stir in ripe olives and sweet pepper. Cover; cook on low-heat setting for 15 minutes more. To serve, spear the dippers with fondue forks and dip into the fondue.

Nutrition Facts per serving: 254 calories, 12 g total fat, 39 mg cholesterol, 738 mg sodium, 24 g carbohydrate, 13 g protein.

4 ounces bulk Italian sausage
1 small onion, finely chopped
1 clove garlic, minced
1 30-ounce jar meatless
   spaghetti sauce
1 cup sliced fresh mushrooms
⅔ cup chopped pepperoni
   or Canadian-style bacon
1 teaspoon dried basil
   or oregano, crushed
½ cup sliced pitted ripe olives
   (optional)
¼ cup chopped green sweet
   pepper (optional)
   Dippers such as focaccia
   bread or Italian bread cubes,
   mozzarella or provolone
   cheese cubes, or cooked
   tortellini or ravioli

Cheeseburger Dip

America's favorite sandwich gets deconstructed in this fun dip. Serve it with cocktail buns for scooping, and you won't miss a thing from the real McCoy.

Prep: 15 minutes **Cook:** 3 hours on low or 1½ hours on high **Makes:** 5½ cups (twenty two, ¼-cup servings)

2 pounds lean ground beef

1½ cups chopped onion

2 cloves garlic, minced

1 15-ounce jar cheese dip

½ cup ketchup

¼ cup yellow mustard

¼ cup sweet pickle relish

Corn chip scoops, tortilla chips, or cocktail buns

1. In a large skillet cook beef, onion, and garlic until meat is brown. Drain off fat.

2. Stir cheese dip, ketchup, mustard, and pickle relish into cooked meat mixture. Transfer meat mixture to a 3½-quart slow cooker. Cover; cook on low-heat setting for 3 to 4 hours or on high-heat setting for 1½ to 2 hours. Serve immediately or keep warm on low-heat setting for up to 2 hours. Serve with chips or buns.

Nutrition Facts per serving: 134 calories, 8 g total fat, 38 mg cholesterol, 447 mg sodium, 5 g carbohydrate, 10 g protein.

Cheesy Beer-Salsa Dip

Small toasted squares of corn bread make the perfect vehicle for enjoying this three-cheese and salsa extravaganza. Choose the level of heat by using either mild, medium, or hot salsa.

Prep: 15 minutes **Cook:** 3 hours on low or 1½ hours on high **Makes:** 5½ cups (twenty two, ¼-cup servings)

1. In a 3½- or 4-quart slow cooker combine salsa, three cheeses, and beer.

2. Cover; cook on low-heat setting for 3 to 4 hours or on high-heat setting for 1½ to 2 hours. Serve immediately or keep warm on low-heat setting for up to 2 hours. Stir before serving. Serve with Corn Bread Dippers or tortilla chips.

Nutrition Facts per serving: 211 calories, 15 g total fat, 47 mg cholesterol, 557 mg sodium, 10 g carbohydrate, 9 g protein.

Corn Bread Dippers: Prepare one 8½-ounce package corn muffin mix according to package directions. Spread in an 8×8×2-inch baking pan and bake in 400°F oven for 20 minutes or until toothpick inserted in center comes out clean. Cool bread in pan on a wire rack for 5 minutes. Remove bread from pan; cool completely. Cut into ½-inch-thick slices; cut each slice into three pieces. Place in single layer on a large baking sheet. Bake in a 425°F oven for 10 minutes or until crisp, turning once. Cool on wire rack. Store in an airtight container up to 2 days. Makes about 42.

1 16-ounce jar salsa

4 cups shredded American cheese (1 pound)

2 cups shredded Monterey Jack cheese or American cheese (8 ounces)

1 8-ounce package cream cheese, cut up

⅔ cup beer or milk

Corn Bread Dippers or tortilla chips

Hot Artichoke Dip

This classic is a surefire hit with any crowd. Serve it on toasted pita wedges or lavosh cracker bread. Clean the leeks thoroughly by slicing them lengthwise and fanning the layers under running water.

Prep: 20 minutes **Cook:** 3 hours on low **Makes:** 5 cups (twenty, ¼-cup servings)

---

2 medium leeks, thinly sliced
   (⅔ cup)
1 tablespoon olive oil
2 14-ounce cans artichoke
   hearts, drained and
   coarsely chopped
2 cups light mayonnaise
   (do not use regular
   mayonnaise)
1 cup chopped red
   sweet pepper
1 cup finely shredded
   Parmesan cheese
1 teaspoon Mediterranean
   seasoning or
   lemon-pepper seasoning
Finely shredded
   Parmesan cheese
Toasted pita wedges

1. In a large skillet cook leeks in hot olive oil over medium heat until tender. Place in a 3½- to 4-quart slow cooker. Stir in the artichoke hearts, light mayonnaise, sweet pepper, 1 cup Parmesan, and seasoning. Cover; cook on low-heat setting for 3 to 4 hours until cheese is melted and mixture is heated through.

2. To serve, stir mixture, sprinkle with additional Parmesan, and keep warm on low-heat setting for up to 1 hour. Serve on toasted pita wedges.

Nutrition Facts per serving: 129 calories, 10 g total fat, 14 mg cholesterol, 361 mg sodium, 6 g carbohydrate, 3 g protein.

Tex-Mex Cheese Dip

If you like your Tex-Mex spicy, use hot salsa and tongue-tingling chorizo sausage—an authentic Mexican sausage fired up by chiles—in place of the ground beef.

Prep: 15 minutes **Cook:** 3 hours on low or 1½ hours on high **Makes:** 6 cups (twenty four, ¼-cup servings)

1. In a skillet cook beef, chicken, onion, and garlic until meat is brown. Drain off fat.

2. Transfer meat mixture to a 3½- or 4-quart slow cooker. Stir in cumin, coriander, and salsa. Cover; cook on low-heat setting for 3 to 4 hours or on high-heat setting for 1½ to 2 hours until heated through.

3. Stir in cheese. Cover; cook on high-heat setting for 5 to 10 minutes or until cheese melts. Serve with chips. The dip may be kept warm in slow cooker up to 2 hours on low-heat setting.

Nutrition Facts per ¼ cup dip without chips: **133 calories, 10 g total fat, 36 mg cholesterol, 341 mg sodium, 2 g carbohydrate, 10 g protein.**

1½ pounds lean ground beef
 or ground raw chicken
 or ground raw turkey
1 cup chopped onion
2 cloves garlic, minced
1 teaspoon ground cumin
1 teaspoon ground coriander
1 12-ounce jar chunky salsa
1 16-ounce package cheese
 with jalapeño peppers
 Tortilla chips or corn chips

Bacon-Horseradish Dip

Lip-tingling horseradish makes this dip a real kick. Use sharp cheddar for the most intense flavor. Save a little prep time by buying precooked and crumbled bacon.

Prep: 25 minutes **Cook:** 4 hours on low or 2 hours on high **Makes:** 5 cups (twenty, ¼-cup servings)

3 8-ounce packages
cream cheese, softened
and cut up

3 cups shredded cheddar
cheese (12 ounces)

1 cup half-and-half
or light cream

⅓ cup chopped green onion

3 tablespoons prepared
horseradish

1 tablespoon Worcestershire
sauce

3 cloves garlic, minced

½ teaspoon coarse ground
black pepper

12 slices bacon, crisp cooked,
cooled, and finely crumbled
(1 cup)

Corn chips, toasted
baguette slices,
toasted pita wedges,
or assorted crackers

1. In a 3½- or 4-quart slow cooker combine cream cheese, cheddar cheese, half-and-half, green onion, horseradish, Worcestershire sauce, garlic, and pepper. Cover; cook on low-heat setting for 4 to 5 hours or on high-heat setting for 2 to 2½ hours, stirring once halfway through cooking. Stir in the bacon. Serve with corn chips, baguette slices, pita wedges, or assorted crackers.

Nutrition Facts per serving: **227 calories, 21 g total fat, 63 mg cholesterol, 282 mg sodium, 2 g carbohydrate, 8 g protein.**

Spicy Sausage Pizza Dip

Deep-dish pizza has nothing on this tasty pot of dip. Stir it occasionally as it's served to keep the sausage evenly distributed throughout the tomato sauce.

Prep: 20 minutes **Cook:** 6 hours on low or 3 hours on high **Makes:** 3½ cups dip (fourteen, ¼-cup servings)

1. In a large skillet cook Italian sausage, onion, and garlic until meat is brown and onion is tender; drain well.

2. In a 3½- or 4-quart slow cooker combine sausage mixture, tomato sauce, tomatoes, tomato paste, oregano, basil, sugar, and red pepper. Stir all ingredients together. Cover; cook on low-heat setting for 6 to 8 hours or on high-heat setting for 3 to 4 hours.

3. Stir in olives. Sprinkle with grated Parmesan cheese. Serve with desired dippers.

Nutrition Facts per serving: **120 calories, 8 g total fat, 22 mg cholesterol, 378 mg sodium, 5 g carbohydrate, 6 g protein.**

- 1 pound bulk Italian sausage
- 1 small onion, chopped (⅓ cup)
- 2 cloves garlic, minced
- 1 15-ounce can tomato sauce
- 1 7½-ounce can tomatoes, undrained and cut up
- ½ of a 6-ounce can tomato paste (⅓ cup)
- 2 teaspoons dried oregano, crushed
- 1½ teaspoons dried basil, crushed
- 1 teaspoon sugar
- ⅛ teaspoon ground red pepper
- ¼ cup chopped black olives
- 2 tablespoons grated Parmesan cheese

  Dippers: breadsticks, breaded mozzarella cheese sticks, and green sweet pepper strips

Asiago Cheese Dip

Keep this creamy, elegant dip warm in a slow cooker for up to two hours after cooking. Stir it just before serving so everyone gets a bit of tomato, mushroom, and green onion in every bite.

Prep: 15 minutes **Cook:** 3 hours on low or 1½ hours on high **Makes:** 7 cups (twenty eight, ¼-cup servings)

---

1 cup chicken broth or water
4 ounces dried tomatoes
4 8-ounce cartons dairy
    sour cream
1¼ cups mayonnaise
½ of an 8-ounce package
    cream cheese, cut up
1 cup sliced fresh mushrooms
1 cup thinly sliced green onion
6 ounces shredded Asiago
    cheese (1½ cups)
Thinly sliced green onion
Toasted baguette slices

1. In a medium saucepan bring the chicken broth or water to boiling. Remove from heat and add the dried tomatoes. Cover and let stand for 5 minutes. Drain, discard the liquid, and chop the tomatoes (about 1¼ cups).

2. Meanwhile, in a 3½- or 4-quart slow cooker combine the sour cream, mayonnaise, cream cheese, mushrooms, 1 cup green onion, and Asiago cheese. Stir in the chopped tomatoes. Cover; cook on low-heat setting for 3 to 4 hours or on high-heat setting for 1½ to 2 hours. Stir before serving and sprinkle with additional green onion. Keep warm on low-heat setting for 1 to 2 hours. Serve warm with toasted baguette slices.

Nutrition Facts per serving: 195 calories, 19 g total fat, 31 mg cholesterol, 242 mg sodium, 5 g carbohydrate, 4 g protein.

Reuben Spread

All the elements of the classic Reuben sandwich—spiced corned beef, tangy sauerkraut, Swiss cheese, and sweet Thousand Island dressing—mingle in this creamy, melted mélange.

Prep: 15 minutes **Cook:** 2½ hours on low **Makes:** 5 cups (twenty, ¼-cup servings)

1. In a 3½- or 4-quart slow cooker combine corned beef, sauerkraut, dressing, cheeses, horseradish, and caraway seed.

2. Cover; cook on low-heat setting for 2½ to 3 hours. Serve immediately or keep warm on low-heat setting for up to 2 hours. Stir well before serving. Serve with toasted bread slices or crackers.

Nutrition Facts per serving: **157 calories, 13 g total fat, 38 mg cholesterol, 531 mg sodium, 3 g carbohydrate, 7 g protein.**

1 pound cooked corned beef, finely chopped

1 16-ounce can sauerkraut, rinsed, drained, and snipped

1 cup Thousand Island salad dressing

1½ cups shredded Swiss cheese (6 ounces)

1 3-ounce package cream cheese, cubed

1 tablespoon prepared horseradish

1 teaspoon caraway seed
Toasted cocktail rye bread slices or rye crackers

Apricot-Glazed Ham Balls

Cut the ham in 1-inch chunks before putting it in a food processor or blender to grind it to a fine texture. You can also ask the meat-counter attendant to grind it for you.

Prep: 20 minutes **Bake:** 20 minutes **Cook:** 4 hours on low or 1½ hours on high **Makes:** 30 meatballs

1 egg, beaten
½ cup graham cracker crumbs
   (7 squares)
2 tablespoons unsweetened
   pineapple juice
1 teaspoon dry mustard
¼ teaspoon salt
½ pound fully
   cooked ham ground
½ pound ground pork
½ cup snipped dried apricots
1 18-ounce jar apricot
   preserves
⅓ cup unsweetened
   pineapple juice
1 tablespoon cider vinegar
½ teaspoon ground ginger

1. For meatballs, in a large bowl combine egg, graham cracker crumbs, the 2 tablespoons pineapple juice, dry mustard, and salt. Add ham, pork, and apricots; mix well. Shape into 30 meatballs. Place in a 15×10×1-inch baking pan. Bake, uncovered, in a 350°F oven for 20 minutes. Remove from oven; drain.

2. Meanwhile, stir together apricot preserves, the ⅓ cup pineapple juice, vinegar, and ginger. Set aside.

3. Add cooked meatballs to 3½- or 4-quart slow cooker. Pour apricot preserve mixture over meatballs. Cover; cook on low-heat setting for 4 to 5 hours or on high-heat setting for 1½ to 2 hours. Serve immediately or cover and keep warm on low-heat setting for up to 2 hours. Gently stir before serving.

Nutrition Facts per meatball: 86 calories, 2 g total fat, 15 mg cholesterol, 151 mg sodium, 15 g carbohydrate, 3 g protein.

Tangy Cocktail Meatballs

If you can't find stuffing mix, use croutons that have been lightly crushed inside a sealable plastic bag with a rolling pin or the bottom of a mixing bowl.

Prep: 20 minutes **Bake:** 15 minutes **Cook:** 2 hours on high **Makes:** 50 meatballs

1. In a large bowl combine egg, soup, stuffing mix, and salt. Add ground beef; mix well. Shape into 1-inch meatballs. Place meatballs in a 15×10×1-inch baking pan. Bake in a 350°F oven for 15 to 18 minutes or until cooked through. Drain meatballs and transfer to a 3½-, 4-, or 5-quart slow cooker.

2. In a bowl combine ketchup, tomato sauce, water, brown sugar, Worcestershire sauce, vinegar, and tapioca. Pour over meatballs; stir gently to coat.

3. Cover; cook on high-heat setting for 2 to 3 hours. Serve immediately or keep warm on low-heat setting up to 2 hours. Serve with toothpicks.

Nutrition Facts per meatball: 58 calories, 3 g total fat, 15 mg cholesterol, 191 mg sodium, 5 g carbohydrate, 4 g protein.

1 egg, beaten
1 10½-ounce can condensed French onion soup
2 cups herb-seasoned stuffing mix
½ teaspoon seasoned salt
2 pounds ground beef
1 cup salsa-style ketchup or regular ketchup
1 8-ounce can tomato sauce
1 cup water
⅓ cup packed brown sugar
¼ cup Worcestershire sauce
¼ cup vinegar
2 tablespoons quick-cooking tapioca

Cranberry-Sauced Sausages

With beautifully hued, sweet-tart cranberry sauce and aromatic allspice, these saucy sausages are just the thing to serve at a casual holiday gathering.

Prep: 10 minutes **Cook:** 2 hours on high **Makes:** 16 servings

---

**2 8-ounce cans jellied
   cranberry sauce**

⅔ cup ketchup

2 tablespoons lemon juice

1 teaspoon dry mustard

¼ teaspoon ground allspice

**2 5.3-ounce packages
   small fully cooked
   smoked sausage links**

In a 3½- or 4-quart slow cooker combine cranberry sauce, ketchup, lemon juice, dry mustard, and allspice. Stir in the sausage links. Cover; cook for about 2 hours on high setting or until heated through.

Nutrition Facts per serving: **119 calories, 6 g total fat, 13 mg cholesterol, 304 mg sodium, 14 g carbohydrate, 3 g protein.**

Sweet 'n' Sour Ham Balls

If you don't have time to make the meatballs, simply stir up the sweet-and-sour sauce and add cocktail wieners or Polish sausage chunks—then cover and heat.

Prep: 30 minutes **Cook:** 4 hours on low or 1½ hours on high **Makes:** 30 meatballs

1. In a 3½- or 4-quart slow cooker stir together sweet-and-sour sauce, pineapple juice, brown sugar, and ground ginger. Set aside.

2. For meatballs, in a large bowl combine egg, graham cracker crumbs, and milk. Add ham and pork; mix well. Shape into 30 meatballs. Spray a 12-inch skillet with cooking spray. Add meatballs and brown on all sides over medium heat.

3. Add browned meatballs to slow cooker. Cover; cook on low-heat setting for 4 to 5 hours or on high-heat setting for 1½ to 2 hours. Serve immediately or keep warm on low-heat setting for up to 2 hours.

Nutrition Facts per meatball: 51 calories, 1 g total fat, 13 mg cholesterol, 130 mg sodium, 7 g carbohydrate, 3 g protein.

1 9- or 10-ounce bottle
   sweet-and-sour sauce
⅓ cup unsweetened
   pineapple juice
⅓ cup packed brown sugar
¼ teaspoon ground ginger
1 egg, beaten
½ cup graham cracker crumbs
2 tablespoons milk
½ pound ground fully
   cooked ham
½ pound ground pork
   Nonstick cooking spray

Hot Honeyed Spareribs

Party hearty with these ribs. They're perfect for an open house. They stay warm in the honeyed picante sauce and no one goes away hungry.

Prep: 20 minutes **Broil:** 10 minutes **Cook:** 6 hours on low or 3 hours on high **Makes:** 10 to 12 servings

3½ to 4 pounds pork baby back ribs, cut into 1-rib portions
2 cups bottled picante sauce or salsa (32 ounces)
½ cup honey
1 tablespoon quick-cooking tapioca
1 teaspoon ground ginger

1. Preheat broiler. Place ribs on the unheated rack of a broiler pan. Broil 6 inches from the heat about 10 minutes or until brown, turning once. Transfer ribs to a 3½-, 4-, 5-, or 6-quart slow cooker.

2. In a medium bowl combine picante sauce, honey, tapioca, and ginger. Pour sauce over ribs.

3. Cover; cook on low-heat setting for 6 to 7 hours or on high-heat setting for 3 to 3½ hours. If desired, skim off fat from sauce. Serve sauce with ribs.

Nutrition Facts per serving: **215 calories, 6 g total fat, 43 mg cholesterol, 246 mg sodium, 18 g carbohydrate, 20 g protein.**

Buffalo Wings with Blue Cheese Dip

Serve these spicy sports-bar favorites with their traditional accompaniments: crisp celery sticks and cold beer. The dip will hold up to two weeks in the refrigerator—if there's any left over.

Prep: 30 minutes **Broil:** 10 minutes **Cook:** 4 hours on low or 2 hours on high **Makes:** 32 servings

1. Preheat broiler. Cut off and discard wing tips. Cut each wing into 2 sections. Place chicken on the unheated rack of a broiler pan. Broil 4 to 5 inches from the heat about 10 minutes or until chicken is browned, turning once. Transfer chicken to a 3½- or 4-quart slow cooker. Combine chili sauce and hot pepper sauce; pour over chicken wings.

2. Cover; cook on low-heat setting for 4 to 5 hours or on high-heat setting for 2 to 2½ hours. Serve chicken wings with Blue Cheese Dip or ranch salad dressing.

Blue Cheese Dip: In a blender container combine one 8-ounce carton dairy sour cream; ½ cup mayonnaise or salad dressing; ½ cup crumbled blue cheese (2 ounces); 1 clove garlic, minced; and 1 tablespoon white wine vinegar or white vinegar. Cover and blend until smooth. Store dip, covered, in the refrigerator for up to 2 weeks. If desired, top dip with additional crumbled blue cheese before serving. Makes 1½ cups.

Nutrition Facts per piece with 1 tablespoon Blue Cheese Dip: 108 calories, 8 g total fat, 21 mg cholesterol, 217 mg sodium, 3 g carbohydrate, 6 g protein.

16 chicken wings (about 3 pounds)
1½ cups bottled chili sauce
3 to 4 tablespoons bottled hot pepper sauce
1 recipe Blue Cheese Dip or bottled ranch salad dressing

Barbecue-Style Chicken Wings

Serve lots of napkins (maybe even some moist towelettes!) with these sweet and saucy wings.

Prep: 15 minutes **Broil:** 10 minutes **Cook:** 4 hours on low or 2 hours on high **Makes:** 32 servings

16 **chicken wings
   (about 3 pounds)**
1½ **cups bottled
    barbecue sauce**
¼ **cup honey**
2 **teaspoons prepared mustard**
1½ **teaspoons Worcestershire
    sauce**

1. Preheat broiler. Cut off and discard wing tips. Cut each wing at joint to make 2 sections.

2. Place chicken on unheated rack of a broiler pan. Broil 4 to 5 inches from the heat about 10 minutes or until chicken is browned, turning once. Transfer to a 3½- or 4-quart slow cooker.

3. For sauce, combine barbecue sauce, honey, mustard, and Worcestershire sauce; pour over chicken wings. Cover; cook on low-heat setting for 4 to 5 hours or on high-heat setting for 2 to 2½ hours.

Nutrition Facts per serving: 67 calories, 4 g total fat, 14 mg cholesterol, 115 mg sodium, 4 g carbohydrate, 5 g protein.

Five-Spice Pecans

The slow cooker toasts nuts to a beautiful golden brown and enhances their flavor. Toast these Asian-flavored nibbles and freeze them in 1- to 2-cup batches up to 3 months before the holidays.

Prep: 10 minutes **Cook:** 2 hours on low and 15 minutes on high **Makes:** 4 cups (sixteen, ¼-cup servings)

1. Place pecans in a 3½- or 4-quart slow cooker. In a bowl combine the melted margarine, soy sauce, five-spice powder, garlic powder, ginger, and red pepper. Pour over nuts. Stir to coat nuts.

2. Cover; cook on low-heat setting for 2 hours. Uncover and stir. Turn to high-heat setting. Cover and continue cooking on high-heat setting for 15 to 30 minutes. Cool.

Nutrition Facts per serving: **217 calories, 22 g total fat, 8 mg cholesterol, 145 mg sodium, 6 g carbohydrate, 2 g protein.**

1 pound pecan halves (4 cups)
¼ cup margarine
or butter, melted
2 tablespoons soy sauce
1 teaspoon five-spice powder
½ teaspoon garlic powder
½ teaspoon ground ginger
¼ teaspoon ground red pepper

soups and stews

*From the lightest soup to enjoy as a starter or alongside
a sandwich to the heartiest stew, your slow cooker keeps food
warm and satisfying as it simmers all day.*

Chicken & White Bean Soup, page 47

Beef and Noodle Soup

Buy the stew meat already cut and there's no chopping needed to make this hearty beef and vegetable soup. Use homemade-style egg noodles to make it especially toothsome.

Prep: 15 minutes **Cook:** 9 hours on low plus 30 minutes on high or 5 hours on high **Makes:** 8 servings

1 pound beef stew meat, cut into ½-inch cubes

1 16-ounce package frozen mixed vegetables

5 cups water

1 14½-ounce can diced tomatoes, undrained

1 8-ounce can tomato sauce

2 bay leaves

2 tablespoons instant beef bouillon granules

1½ teaspoons dried basil, crushed

½ teaspoon dried marjoram, crushed

¼ teaspoon ground black pepper

2 cups uncooked medium noodles

1. In a 4½-, 5- or 6-quart slow cooker combine meat, frozen mixed vegetables, water, tomatoes, tomato sauce, bay leaves, bouillon granules, basil, marjoram, and pepper.

2. Cover and cook on low-heat setting for 9 to 11 hours or on high-heat setting for 4½ to 5½ hours.

3. If using low-heat setting, turn to high-heat setting. Stir in noodles. Cover; cook for 30 minutes more. Remove and discard bay leaves.

Nutrition Facts per serving: **179 calories, 4 g total fat, 36 mg cholesterol, 1,106 mg sodium, 19 g carbohydrate, 17 g protein.**

Beef and Spinach Soup with Rice

This soup is good made with lamb too. Simply substitute the beef with lamb stew meat and exchange the thyme and basil for ¾ teaspoon dried rosemary and ¾ teaspoon dried mint.

Prep: 25 minutes **Cook:** 8 hours on low or 4 hours on high. Stand: 5 minutes **Makes:** 8 servings

1. Trim off fat from meat. In a large skillet brown meat, half at a time, in hot oil. Drain off the fat.

2. In a 3½-, 4-, or 5-quart slow cooker place carrots, squash, onion, garlic, thyme, and basil. Place meat on top of vegetables. Pour broth and wine, if desired, over all.

3. Cover; cook on low-heat setting for 8 to 10 hours or on high-heat setting for 4 to 5 hours.

4. Stir in spinach and rice. Cover and let stand 5 to 10 minutes or until rice is tender.

Nutrition Facts per serving: **213 calories, 8 g total fat, 62 mg cholesterol, 693 mg sodium, 11 g carbohydrate, 25 g protein.**

1½ pounds beef stew meat, cut into 1-inch cubes
1 tablespoon cooking oil
2 medium carrots, cut into ½-inch slices (1 cup)
2 medium yellow summer squash, halved lengthwise, and cut into ½-inch slices (2½ cups)
1 cup chopped onion
1 clove garlic, minced
¾ teaspoon dried thyme, crushed
¾ teaspoon dried basil, crushed
6 cups beef broth
¼ cup dry red or white wine (optional)
2 cups chopped fresh spinach
½ cup instant rice

Beef-Barley Soup

Just a little bit of spaghetti sauce adds a nice tomato flavor and rosy hue to this homey soup.

Prep: 25 minutes **Cook:** 10 hours on low or 4½ hours on high **Makes:** 6 to 8 servings

1½ pounds beef stew meat cut
    into 1-inch cubes
1 tablespoon cooking oil
1 cup thinly sliced carrots
1 cup sliced celery
1 medium onion, thinly sliced
½ cup coarsely chopped green
    sweet pepper
¼ cup snipped fresh parsley
4 cups beef broth
1 14½-ounce can tomatoes,
    undrained and cut up
1 cup spaghetti sauce
⅔ cup pearl barley
1½ teaspoons dried basil,
    crushed
1 teaspoon salt
¼ teaspoon ground black
    pepper

1. In a large skillet brown meat, half at a time, in hot oil. Drain well. Meanwhile, in a 3½-, 4-, 5-, or 6-quart slow cooker combine carrots, celery, onion, green sweet pepper, and parsley. Add broth, tomatoes, spaghetti sauce, barley, basil, salt, and pepper. Stir in browned meat.

2. Cover; cook on low-heat setting for 10 to 12 hours or on high-heat setting for 4½ to 5 hours. Skim off fat.

Nutrition Facts per serving: **395 calories, 18 g total fat, 73 mg cholesterol, 1,225 mg sodium, 30 g carbohydrate, 29 g protein.**

Italian Wedding Soup

Italian wedding soup gets its name from the marriage of meat and greens. You can use ground beef, pork, or lamb—depending on your personal preferences.

Prep: 20 minutes   **Cook:** 8¼ hours on low or 4¼ hours on high   **Makes:** 6 servings

1. Finely chop three of the cipollini. Combine cipollini, ground beef, tomatoes, and 1½ teaspoons of the Italian seasoning in a large bowl. Divide mixture and roll into 12 balls about an inch in diameter. Brown meatballs in a large, nonstick skillet brushed lightly with cooking oil. Transfer to a 4- or 5-quart slow cooker.

2. Trim fennel and cut into wedges, reserving several of the leafy fronds for garnish, if desired. Place remaining six cipollini, fennel wedges, garlic, broth, remaining 1½ teaspoons Italian seasoning, and pepper in the slow cooker.

3. Cover; cook on low-heat setting for 8 to 10 hours or on high-heat setting for 4 to 5 hours.

4. Gently stir in spinach and orzo; cover and cook 15 minutes more. Serve in deep bowls and, if desired, top with reserved fennel fronds.

Nutrition Facts per serving: **172 calories, 6 g total fat, 27 mg cholesterol, 908 mg sodium, 17 g carbohydrate, 13 g protein.**

- 9 cipollini or boiling onions, peeled
- 12 ounces lean ground beef
- 2 oil-packed dried tomatoes, minced
- 1 tablespoon dried Italian seasoning, crushed
- 1 large fennel bulb
- 4 cloves garlic, chopped
- 3 14-ounce cans chicken broth
- ¼ teaspoon coarsely ground white pepper
- 5 cups shredded fresh spinach
- 1½ cups cooked orzo pasta

Zesty Beef and Vegetable Soup

Hot-style vegetable juice gives this soup a bit of zing. Round out the meal with some warm corn bread.

Prep: 25 minutes **Cook:** 8 hours on low or 4 hours on high **Makes:** 6 servings

1 pound ground beef

½ cup chopped onion

2 cloves garlic, minced

2 cups preshredded coleslaw mix

1 10-ounce package frozen whole kernel corn

1 9-ounce package frozen cut green beans

4 cups hot-style vegetable juice

1 14½-ounce can Italian-style stewed tomatoes, undrained

2 tablespoons Worcestershire sauce

1 teaspoon dried basil, crushed

¼ teaspoon ground black pepper

1. In a large skillet cook ground beef, onion, and garlic until meat is brown and onion is tender. Drain off fat.

2. In a 3½-, 4-, or 5-quart slow cooker combine meat mixture, coleslaw mix, corn, beans, vegetable juice, tomatoes, Worcestershire sauce, basil, and pepper.

3. Cover; cook on low-heat setting for 8 to 10 hours or on high-heat setting for 4 to 5 hours.

Nutrition Facts per serving: **269 calories, 10 g total fat, 48 mg cholesterol, 925 mg sodium, 29 g carbohydrate, 19 g protein.**

Beef 'n' Brew Vegetable Soup

A can of ale adds flavor to this beefy soup. Use a light beer for just a touch of beer taste; use a dark beer for a more intense taste.

Prep: 20 minutes **Cook:** 10 hours on low or 5 hours on high **Makes:** 6 servings

1. In a 5- or 6-quart slow cooker place onions, carrots, parsnips, garlic, bay leaves, dried thyme (if using), and pepper. Sprinkle with tapioca. Place meat on top of vegetables. Add beef broth and beer.

2. Cover; cook on low-heat setting for 10 to 12 hours or on high-heat setting for 5 to 6 hours. To serve, remove bay leaves; stir in fresh thyme, if using.

Nutrition Facts per serving: 354 calories, 9 g total fat, 82 mg cholesterol, 336 mg sodium, 35 g carbohydrate, 31 g protein.

3 medium onions, sliced
1 pound carrots, cut into ½-inch slices
4 parsnips, cut into ½-inch slices
4 cloves garlic, minced
2 bay leaves
1 tablespoon snipped fresh thyme or 1 teaspoon dried thyme, crushed
½ teaspoon ground black pepper
2 tablespoons quick-cooking tapioca
1½ pounds beef stew meat, cut into 1-inch cubes
1 14-ounce can beef broth
1 12-ounce can beer

Ham and Black-Eyed Pea Soup

Ten minutes of boiling on the stovetop gives the black-eyed peas a head start on the rest of the soup ingredients and ensures they'll be tender at serving time.

Prep: 20 minutes **Cook:** 11 hours on low or 4½ hours on high **Makes:** 6 servings

---

5½ cups water

12 ounces dry black-eyed peas
   or navy beans (2 cups)

2 14½-ounce cans reduced-
   sodium chicken broth

1 cup reduced-sodium ham,
   cut into ½-inch pieces

4 medium carrots, sliced
   ½ inch thick (2 cups)

2 stalks celery, sliced (1 cup)

¼ cup dried minced onion

1 teaspoon dried sage,
   crushed

1 teaspoon dried thyme,
   crushed

¼ teaspoon ground red pepper

1 tablespoon lemon juice

1. Bring 4 cups of the water and black-eyed peas to boiling in a 3-quart saucepan. Boil, uncovered, for 10 minutes. Drain and rinse.

2. In a 4-quart slow cooker combine broth, ham, carrots, celery, onion, sage, thyme, red pepper, and the remaining 1½ cups water. Stir in peas or beans.

3. Cover; cook on low-heat setting for 11 to 12 hours or on high-heat setting for 4½ to 5½ hours. To serve, stir in lemon juice.

Nutrition Facts per serving: 251 calories, 3 g total fat, 12 mg cholesterol, 753 mg sodium, 41 g carbohydrate, 19 g protein.

Calico Ham and Bean Soup

Use a pound of purchased bean mix or a pound of any one kind of bean to make this soup. It won't be "calico," but it will taste just as good. If you like a thicker soup, mash some of the beans before serving.

Prep: 20 minutes **Cook:** 8 hours on low or 4 hours on high **Makes:** 8 servings

1. Rinse beans; drain. In a large saucepan combine the beans, peas, and the 6 cups of the water. Bring to boiling; reduce heat. Simmer, uncovered, for 10 minutes. Drain and rinse beans.

2. Meanwhile, in a 3½-, 4-, or 5-quart slow cooker combine ham, onion, carrot, basil, oregano, ¾ teaspoon salt, ¼ teaspoon pepper, and bay leaves. Stir in drained beans and the remaining 6 cups fresh water.

3. Cover; cook on low-heat setting for 8 to 10 hours or on high-heat setting for 4 to 5 hours. Discard the bay leaves. Season to taste with additional salt and pepper.

Nutrition Facts per serving: **244 calories, 3 g total fat, 11 mg cholesterol, 696 mg sodium, 36 g carbohydrate, 19 g protein.**

- ½ cup dry navy or Great Northern beans
- ½ cup dry black beans or kidney beans
- ½ cup dry lima beans
- ½ cup dry garbanzo beans
- ½ cup dry split peas
- 12 cups water
- 2 cups fully cooked ham, cut into ½-inch pieces (about 10 ounces)
- 1 cup chopped onion
- 1 cup chopped carrot
- 1 teaspoon dried basil, crushed
- 1 teaspoon dried oregano, crushed
- ¾ teaspoon salt
- ¼ teaspoon ground black pepper
- 2 bay leaves
  Salt
  Ground black pepper

Autumn Harvest Soup

If you've only heard about parsnips in the tale "Peter Rabbit," taste what made Mr. MacGregor defend his garden so vigorously. Look for firm, small to medium parsnips that have smooth skin.

Prep: 25 minutes **Cook:** 7 hours on low or 3½ hours on high **Makes:** 4 servings

1 pound boneless pork
   shoulder

2 cups cubed, peeled sweet
   potatoes

2 medium parsnips, peeled
   and cut into ½-inch pieces
   (1¾ cups)

2 small cooking apples, cored
   and cut into ¼-inch slices
   (1¾ cups)

1 medium onion, chopped

¾ teaspoon dried thyme,
   crushed

½ teaspoon dried rosemary,
   crushed

½ teaspoon salt

¼ teaspoon ground black
   pepper

2 cups apple cider
   or apple juice

1. Trim fat from meat. Cut pork into 1-inch cubes.

2. In a 3½- or 4-quart slow cooker layer potatoes, parsnips, apples, and onion. Sprinkle with thyme, rosemary, salt, and pepper. Add meat. Pour apple cider over all.

3. Cover; cook on low-heat setting for 7 to 8 hours or on high-heat setting for 3½ to 4 hours or until meat and vegetables are tender.

Nutrition Facts per serving: **365 calories, 8 g total fat, 76 mg cholesterol, 392 mg sodium, 37 g carbohydrate, 24 g protein.**

Sausage-Sauerkraut Soup

For a garnish that adds both color and flavor to this hearty soup, sprinkle each bowl with a little bit of crumbled crisp-cooked bacon and chopped hard-cooked egg.

Prep: 15 minutes **Cook:** 10 hours on low or 4½ hours on high **Makes:** 4 servings

1. In a 3½-, 4-, 5-, or 6-quart slow cooker combine chicken, Polish sausage, potato, carrot, onion, and celery. Add mushroom soup, sauerkraut, mushrooms, vinegar, dill, and pepper. Stir in chicken broth.

2. Cover; cook on low-heat setting for 10 to 12 hours or on high-heat setting for 4½ to 5½ hours.

Nutrition Facts per serving: 451 calories, 27 g total fat, 91 mg cholesterol, 2,070 mg sodium, 20 g carbohydrate, 31 g protein.

1½ cups chopped cooked chicken
8 ounces smoked Polish sausage links, chopped
1 small potato, cut into ½-inch pieces (¾ cup)
1 medium carrot, cut into ½-inch pieces (½ cup)
½ cup chopped onion
½ cup sliced celery
1 10¾-ounce can condensed cream of mushroom soup
1 8-ounce can sauerkraut, rinsed and drained
1 4-ounce can mushroom stems and pieces, undrained
1 tablespoon vinegar
1 teaspoon dried dill
¼ teaspoon ground black pepper
2½ cups chicken broth

Sausage-Escarole Soup

If you can't find escarole, substitute spinach, curly endive, or another mildly bitter green.

Prep: 30 minutes **Cook:** 8 hours on low or 4 hours on high **Makes:** 6 servings

1 egg, beaten
2 tablespoons milk
¼ cup fine dry bread crumbs
1 pound bulk Italian sausage
Nonstick cooking spray
2 15-ounce cans Great
Northern beans, rinsed and
drained
2 medium carrots, cut into
½-inch pieces (1 cup)
2 medium tomatoes, chopped
½ cup chopped onion
2 cloves garlic, minced
1 teaspoon dried Italian
seasoning, crushed
½ teaspoon crushed
red pepper
5 cups chicken broth
4 cups chopped escarole
Grated Parmesan cheese

1. For meatballs, in a large bowl combine egg, milk, and bread crumbs. Add sausage and mix well. Shape into 1-inch meatballs. Spray a 12-inch skillet with cooking spray. Add meatballs and brown on all sides over medium heat. Drain meatballs.

2. In a 3½-, 4-, or 5-quart slow cooker place beans, carrots, tomatoes, onion, garlic, Italian seasoning, and red pepper. Add meatballs to cooker. Pour broth over all.

3. Cover; cook on low-heat setting for 8 to 10 hours or on high-heat setting for 4 to 5 hours. Stir in escarole. Ladle into bowls. Sprinkle with Parmesan cheese.

Nutrition Facts per serving: **383 calories, 19 g total fat, 83 mg cholesterol, 1,531 mg sodium, 32 g carbohydrate, 28 g protein.**

Split Pea and Ham Soup

A little rice gives this beautiful green soup body and texture in each hearty bite.

Prep: 15 minutes **Cook:** 10 hours on high or 4 hours on low **Stand:** 5 minutes **Makes:** 6 servings

1. In a 3½-, 4-, or 5-quart slow cooker combine ham, peas, onion, celery, carrot, parsley, thyme, and pepper. Pour chicken broth and water over all.

2. Cover; cook on low-heat setting for 10 to 12 hours or on high-heat setting for 4 to 5 hours. Stir in rice. Cover; let stand 5 minutes or until rice is tender.

Nutrition Facts per serving: **256 calories, 4 g total fat, 15 mg cholesterol, 1,097 mg sodium, 35 g carbohydrate, 21 g protein.**

2 cups cubed fully cooked ham (about 10 ounces)
1 cup dry split peas
1 cup chopped onion
1 cup chopped celery with leaves
1 cup shredded carrot
2 tablespoons snipped fresh parsley
½ teaspoon dried thyme, crushed
¼ teaspoon ground black pepper
4 cups chicken broth
2 cups water
1 cup instant rice

Tuscan Sausage and Bean Soup

When you turn on the slow cooker, move the frozen spinach to the refrigerator to thaw.

All you have to do hours later is stir in the spinach and scoop up the soup.

Prep: 25 minutes **Cook:** 11 hours on low **Makes:** 4 to 5 servings

1¼ cups dry Great Northern
   beans

8 cups cold water

12 ounces fresh Italian sausage
   links, cut into ½-inch slices

1¾ cups beef broth

½ cup chopped onion

1 clove garlic, minced

½ teaspoon dried Italian
   seasoning, crushed

1 medium yellow summer
   squash or zucchini,
   sliced (2 cups)

1 14½-ounce can Italian-style
   tomatoes, undrained and
   cut up

⅓ cup dry red wine or water

½ of a 10-ounce package
   frozen chopped spinach,
   thawed and well drained
   Grated Parmesan cheese
   (optional)

1. Rinse beans. In a large saucepan or Dutch oven combine beans and 4 cups of the cold water. Boil, uncovered, for 10 minutes; drain.

2. Meanwhile, in a medium skillet cook Italian sausage until brown. Drain well on paper towels. In a 3½- or 4-quart slow cooker combine the drained beans, remaining 4 cups water, beef broth, onion, garlic, Italian seasoning, Italian sausage, squash, tomatoes, and red wine. Cook, covered, on low heat setting for 11 to 12 hours or until beans are tender.

3. Just before serving, stir spinach into soup. If desired, sprinkle each serving with Parmesan cheese.

Nutrition Facts per serving: **516 calories, 20 g total fat, 57 mg cholesterol, 1,104 mg sodium, 46 g carbohydrate, 28 g protein.**

Lamb and Barley Soup

Browning the lamb half at a time ensures that each piece will sear nicely and have good flavor. Trying to brown all of the meat at once would result in its stewing in its own juices.

Prep: 25 minutes **Cook:** 8 hours on low or 4 hours high **Makes:** 8 servings

1. In a large skillet brown lamb, half at a time, in hot oil. Drain fat.

2. In a 3½-, 4-, or 5-quart slow cooker place meat, mushrooms, barley, onion, carrot, parsnip, undrained tomatoes, garlic, marjoram, salt, pepper, and bay leaf. Pour beef broth over all.

3. Cover; cook on low-heat setting for 8 to 10 hours or on high-heat setting for 4 to 5 hours. Discard bay leaf.

Nutrition Facts per serving: **255 calories, 12 g total fat, 48 mg cholesterol, 854 mg sodium, 21 g carbohydrate, 17 g protein.**

1½ pounds lamb stew meat,
    cut into 1-inch cubes
1 tablespoon cooking oil
2 cups sliced fresh mushrooms
½ cup pearl barley
1 cup chopped onion
1 medium carrot, cut into
    ½-inch pieces (½ cup)
1 large parsnip, peeled and
    cut into ½-inch pieces (¾
    cup)
1 14½-ounce can Italian-style
    stewed tomatoes, undrained
2 cloves garlic, minced
1 teaspoon dried marjoram,
    crushed
½ teaspoon salt
¼ teaspoon ground black
    pepper
1 bay leaf
5 cups beef broth

Lamb, Lentil, and Onion Soup

Crushing dried herbs before adding them to a recipe releases their fragrance and flavor. Measure out the herb into the palm of your hand and rub it between your fingers as you add it to the cooker.

Prep: 25 minutes **Cook:** 7 hours on low or 3½ hours on high **Makes:** 4 to 5 servings

12 ounces lean boneless lamb or beef, cut into ½-inch cubes

1 tablespoon cooking oil

1 cup thinly sliced celery

1 cup coarsely chopped carrot

1 cup dry lentils, rinsed and drained

1 10½-ounce can condensed French onion soup

1 to 1½ teaspoons dried thyme, crushed

¼ teaspoon ground black pepper

3¼ cups water

1. In a large skillet brown meat in hot oil. Meanwhile, in a 3½- or 4-quart slow cooker place celery, carrot, and lentils. Top with browned meat.

2. In a large bowl combine soup, thyme, and pepper. Gradually stir in water; add soup mixture to slow cooker. Cover; cook on low-heat setting for 7 to 8 hours or on high-heat setting for 3½ to 4 hours.

Nutrition Facts per serving: 376 calories, 10 g total fat, 57 mg cholesterol, 693 mg sodium, 38 g carbohydrate, 33 g protein.

Chicken and White Bean Soup

If you prefer a meatless variety, just omit the chicken from this Northern Italian style soup. Garnish each bowl with a few sprinkles of minced fennel fronds (the leafy top of the bulb).

Prep: 20 minutes **Stand:** 1 hour **Cook:** 8 hours on low plus 30 minutes on high or 4½ hours on high **Makes:** 4 to 6 servings

1. Rinse beans; drain. In a large saucepan combine beans and the water. Bring to boiling; reduce heat. Simmer, uncovered, for 2 minutes. Remove from heat. Cover and let stand for 1 hour. (Or skip the boiling step and soak beans overnight in a covered pan.) Drain and rinse beans.

2. Meanwhile, in a 3½-, 4-, or 5-quart slow cooker combine onion, fennel, carrots, garlic, parsley, thyme, marjoram, and pepper. Place beans on top of the vegetables. Pour chicken broth over all.

3. Cover; cook on low-heat setting for 8 to 10 hours or on high-heat setting for 4 to 5 hours.

4. If using low-heat setting, turn to high-heat setting. Stir in chicken and tomatoes. Cover; cook for 30 minutes longer or until heated through.

Nutrition Facts per serving: 471 calories, 13 g total fat, 74 mg cholesterol, 1,250 mg sodium, 46 g carbohydrate, 44 g protein.

- 1 cup dry Great Northern beans
- 6 cups water
- 1 cup chopped onion
- 1 medium fennel bulb, trimmed and cut into ½-inch pieces
- 2 medium carrots, chopped
- 2 cloves garlic, minced
- 2 tablespoons snipped fresh parsley
- 1 teaspoon dried thyme, crushed
- 1 teaspoon dried marjoram, crushed
- ¼ teaspoon ground black pepper
- 4½ cups chicken broth
- 2½ cups chopped cooked chicken
- 1 14½-ounce can stewed tomatoes, undrained

Wild Rice and Chicken Soup

To make precooked chicken, place 12 ounces of chicken breasts in a skillet with 1½ cups water. Bring to boiling and reduce heat. Cover and simmer for 12 to 14 minutes or until chicken is no longer pink.

Prep: 15 minutes **Cook:** 6 hours on low or 3 hours on high **Makes:** 8 to 10 servings

1 10¾-ounce can condensed
    cream of mushroom soup
    or cream of chicken soup
2½ cups chopped
    cooked chicken
2 cups sliced fresh
    mushrooms
1 cup coarsely shredded
    carrot
1 cup sliced celery
1 6-ounce package long grain
    and wild rice mix
5 cups chicken broth
5 cups water

1. In a 5- or 6-quart slow cooker combine soup, chicken, mushrooms, carrot, celery, rice, and contents of seasoning packet from rice mix. Gradually stir in broth and water.

2. Cover; cook on low-heat setting for 6 hours or on high-heat setting for 3 hours.

Nutrition Facts per serving: 241 calories, 7 g total fat, 46 mg cholesterol, 1,237 mg sodium, 24 g carbohydrate, 21 g protein.

Deviled Chicken Soup

The word "deviled" refers to a food seasoned with fiery flavorings such as black pepper, hot pepper sauce, or, as in this soup, mustard. Add more or less to your liking.

Prep: 20 minutes **Cook:** 8 hours on low or 4 hours on high **Makes:** 6 servings

---

1. Cut chicken into bite-size pieces.

2. In a 3½- or 4-quart slow cooker combine the chicken, potato, corn, onion, celery, mustard, pepper, and garlic powder. Pour vegetable juice and chicken broth over all.

3. Cover; cook on low-heat setting for 8 to 10 hours or on high-heat setting for 4 to 5 hours.

Nutrition Facts per serving: **192 calories, 5 g total fat, 36 mg cholesterol, 800 mg sodium, 23 g carbohydrate, 15 g protein.**

- **1 pound skinless, boneless chicken thighs**
- **1 large red potato, chopped**
- **½ of a 16-ounce package frozen whole kernel corn (1½ cups)**
- **1 medium onion, chopped**
- **½ cup chopped celery**
- **3 tablespoons Dijon-style mustard**
- **¼ teaspoon ground black pepper**
- **⅛ teaspoon garlic powder**
- **2½ cups vegetable juice**
- **1 14½-ounce can reduced-sodium chicken broth**

Chicken Tortilla Soup

If you like your soup steaming and spicy hot, top this south-of-the-border bowl with hot pepper cheese.

Prep: 20 minutes **Cook:** 8 hours on low plus 15 minutes on high or 4¼ hours on high **Makes:** 8 servings

1 14½-ounce can diced
   tomatoes, undrained
1 14-ounce can beef broth
2 cups water
1 8-ounce can tomato sauce
½ cup chopped onion
1 4-ounce can chopped green
   chile peppers, drained
1 teaspoon ground cumin
1 teaspoon chili powder
1 teaspoon Worcestershire
   sauce
½ teaspoon garlic powder
1 9-ounce package frozen
   cooked Southwestern flavor
   chicken breast strips,
   thawed
8 to 10 corn tortillas, torn
   into 1- to 2-inch pieces
3 ounces cheddar cheese
   or Monterey Jack cheese
   with jalapeño peppers,
   shredded (¾ cup)

1. In a 3½- or 4-quart slow cooker combine tomatoes, broth, water, tomato sauce, onion, chile peppers, cumin, chili powder, Worcestershire sauce, and garlic powder.

2. Cover; cook on low-heat setting for 8 to 10 hours or on high-heat setting for 4 to 5 hours. If using low-heat setting, turn to high-heat setting. Stir in chicken strips. Cover; cook for 15 minutes more. Stir in tortillas and serve immediately. Garnish each serving with shredded cheese.

Nutrition Facts per serving: **189 calories, 6 g total fat, 26 mg cholesterol, 615 mg sodium, 22 g carbohydrate, 13 g protein.**

Thai Chicken Soup

Lemon grass gives this Asian soup a lemony flavor and fragrance. Look for it in the produce section with the other fresh herbs—it looks like a very large green onion. Use only the fibrous white bulb.

Prep: 20 minutes **Cook:** 6 hours on low or 3 hours on high **Stand:** 5 minutes **Makes:** 6 servings

1. In a 3½-, 4-, or 5-quart slow cooker combine the chicken, broth, carrots, onion, ginger, garlic, lemon grass, and red pepper.

2. Cover; cook on low-heat setting for 6 to 7 hours or on high-heat setting for 3 to 3½ hours. If necessary, skim off fat. Stir coconut milk, pepper, mushrooms, and cilantro into chicken mixture. Cover; let stand 5 to 10 minutes. Remove and discard lemon grass (if using). Ladle soup into bowls. Sprinkle peanuts over each serving.

Nutrition Facts per serving: 328 calories, 20 g total fat, 40 mg cholesterol, 764 mg sodium, 15 g carbohydrate, 23 g protein.

1 pound skinless, boneless chicken breasts or thighs, cut into ¾-inch pieces

4 cups chicken broth

2 cups bias-sliced carrots

1 large onion, chopped

2 tablespoons grated ginger

3 cloves garlic, minced

2 stalks lemon grass, cut into 1-inch pieces, or 1 teaspoon finely shredded lemon peel

½ teaspoon crushed red pepper

1 15-ounce can unsweetened coconut milk

1 pepper, cut into ½-inch pieces

2 4-ounce cans straw or button mushrooms, drained

¼ cup snipped cilantro

⅓ cup chopped roasted peanuts

Split Pea & Smoked Turkey Soup

Adding dry herbs to a soup as it cooks allows them to fully impart their flavor to the mix; adding fresh herbs right before serving prevents them from losing all of their flavor by getting overcooked.

Prep: 20 minutes **Cook:** 6 hours on low or 3 hours on high **Stand:** 10 minutes **Makes:** 6 to 8 servings

2 cups dry yellow split peas
(1 pound)

2 cups chopped cooked
smoked turkey or sliced
cooked turkey sausage

1½ cups coarsely shredded
carrots

1 cup chopped chives

1 clove garlic, minced

1 tablespoon snipped fresh
basil or 1 teaspoon
dried basil, crushed

1 tablespoon snipped fresh
oregano or 1 teaspoon
dried oregano, crushed

5 cups chicken broth

2 cups water

½ cup snipped dried tomatoes
(not oil-packed)

1. Rinse split peas; drain.

2. In a 3½- or 4-quart slow cooker combine the split peas, turkey, carrot, chive, garlic, and dried basil and oregano (if using). Pour chicken broth and water over all.

3. Cover; cook on low-heat setting for 6 to 8 hours or on high-heat setting for 3 to 4 hours. Stir in dried tomatoes; cover and let stand for 10 minutes. If using, stir in fresh basil and oregano.

Nutrition Facts per serving: 204 calories, 2 g total fat, 22 mg cholesterol, 1,313 mg sodium, 26 g carbohydrate, 22 g protein.

Asian Turkey and Rice Soup

If your soup-making time will be short in the morning, cut up the turkey and vegetables the night before and store them in the refrigerator in separate plastic bags.

Prep: 25 minutes **Cook:** 8 hours on low or 4 hours on high **Stand:** 5 minutes **Makes:** 6 servings

1. In a 3½- or 4-quart slow cooker place mushrooms, bok choy, onion, and carrots. Add turkey to cooker. Combine chicken broth, soy sauce, sesame oil (if desired), garlic, and ginger. Pour over vegetables and turkey.

2. Cover; cook on low-heat setting for 8 to 10 hours or on high-heat setting for 4 to 5 hours. Stir in rice. Cover and let stand 5 to 10 minutes.

Nutrition Facts per serving: **186 calories, 1 g total fat, 47 mg cholesterol, 584 mg sodium, 20 g carbohydrate, 24 g protein.**

2 cups sliced fresh mushrooms, such as shiitake or button

1½ cups sliced bok choy

1 medium onion, chopped

2 medium carrots, cut into bite-size strips (1 cup)

1 pound turkey breast tenderloins or skinless, boneless chicken breast halves, cut into 1-inch pieces

2 14½-ounce cans reduced-sodium chicken broth

2 tablespoons reduced-sodium soy sauce

1 tablespoon toasted sesame oil (optional)

4 cloves garlic, minced

2 teaspoons grated fresh ginger

1 cup instant rice

French Onion Soup

Pair this French bistro classic with a leafy green salad, some crusty bread, and a glass of wine.

Prep: 30 minutes **Cook:** 5 hours on low or 2½ hours on high **Makes:** 6 to 8 servings

4 to 6 onions, thinly sliced
   (4 to 6 cups)
1 clove garlic, minced
3 tablespoons margarine
   or butter
3 10½-ounce cans condensed
   beef broth
1 cup water
1½ teaspoons Worcestershire
   sauce
⅛ teaspoon ground bkack
   pepper
6 to 8 1-inch slices
   French bread
6 to 8 ¾-ounce slices
   Swiss or Gruyère cheese

1. In a large skillet cook onions and garlic in hot margarine, covered, over medium-low heat about 20 minutes or until tender, stirring occasionally.

2. Transfer onion mixture to a 3½- or 4-quart slow cooker. Add beef broth, water, Worcestershire sauce, and pepper. Cover; cook on low-heat setting for 5 to 10 hours or on high-heat setting for 2½ to 3 hours.

3. Preheat broiler. Before serving soup, toast bread slices. Then arrange toast slices on a baking sheet and top each with a slice of cheese; broil 3 to 4 inches from the heat for 3 to 4 minutes or until cheese is light brown and bubbly. Ladle soup into bowls; top with toast.

For 5- or 6-quart slow cooker: Use 6 to 8 onions, thinly sliced; 1 clove garlic, minced; ¼ cup margarine or butter; four 10½-ounce cans condensed beef broth; 1½ cups water; 2 teaspoons Worcestershire sauce; ⅛ teaspoon ground black pepper; 10 to 12 slices French bread; and 10 to 12 slices Swiss or Gruyère cheese. Prepare as above. Makes 10 to 12 servings.

Nutrition Facts per serving: 256 calories, 12 g total fat, 19 mg cholesterol, 1,064 mg sodium, 21 g carbohydrate, 15 g protein.

Tomato-Rice Soup with Pesto

Look for prepared pesto on the grocery shelf or in the refrigerator section near the fresh pastas.

Prep: 15 minutes **Cook:** 8 hours on low or 4 hours on high **Stand:** 6 minutes **Makes:** 6 servings

1. In a 3½- or 4-quart slow cooker combine onion, carrot, celery, tomatoes, tomato paste, oregano, thyme, and pepper. Stir in water and chicken broth.

2. Cover; cook on low-heat setting for 8 to 10 hours or on high-heat setting for 4 to 5 hours.

3. Stir in rice. Cover; let stand 6 to 7 minutes or until rice is tender. Stir in pesto. Ladle soup into bowls. If desired, sprinkle with grated Parmesan cheese.

Nutrition Facts per serving: **229 calories, 8 g total fat, 2 mg cholesterol, 876 mg sodium, 33 g carbohydrate, 7 g protein.**

1 cup chopped onion
1 cup shredded carrot
3 stalks celery with leaves, chopped
1 14½-ounce can Italian-style stewed tomatoes, undrained
1 6-ounce can Italian-style tomato paste
½ teaspoon dried oregano, crushed
¼ teaspoon dried thyme, crushed
¼ teaspoon ground black pepper
2 cups water
2 cups chicken broth or vegetable broth
1 cup instant rice
¼ cup pesto
  Grated Parmesan cheese (optional)

Hot-and-Sour Soup

Use a whisk to stir the soup as you add the beaten egg to ensure it forms strands of cooked egg.

Prep: 20 minutes **Cook:** 9 hours 50 minutes on low or 3 hours 50 minutes on high **Makes:** 8 servings

4 cups chicken broth

1 8-ounce can bamboo shoots, drained

1 8-ounce can sliced water chestnuts, drained

1 6-ounce can sliced mushrooms, drained

3 tablespoons quick-cooking tapioca

3 tablespoons rice wine vinegar or vinegar

1 tablespoon soy sauce

1 teaspoon sugar

½ teaspoon ground black pepper

1 8-ounce package frozen peeled and deveined shrimp

4 ounces firm tofu (fresh bean curd), drained and cubed

1 egg, beaten

2 tablespoons snipped fresh parsley or cilantro

1. In a 3½- or 4-quart slow cooker combine broth, bamboo shoots, water chestnuts, mushrooms, tapioca, vinegar, soy sauce, sugar, and pepper. Cover; cook on low-heat setting for 9 to 11 hours or on high-heat setting for 3 to 4 hours. Add shrimp and tofu. Cover; cook on low- or high-heat setting for 50 minutes more.

2. Pour the beaten egg slowly into the soup in a thin stream. Stir the soup gently so the egg forms fine shreds instead of clumps. Top with parsley.

Nutrition Facts per serving: **114 calories, 2 g total fat, 83 mg cholesterol, 664 mg sodium, 9 g carbohydrate, 13 g protein.**

Black Bean Soup

If you soak the dry beans in water overnight, you can skip the precooking step.

Prep: 25 minutes **Stand:** 1 hour **Cook:** 12 hours on low or 6 hours on high **Makes:** 6 to 8 servings

1. Rinse beans; place in a large saucepan. Add 6 cups of the cold water. Bring to boiling; reduce heat. Simmer, uncovered, for 10 minutes. Remove from heat. Cover and let stand for 1 hour. Drain and rinse beans.

2. In a 4-, 5-, or 5½-quart slow cooker combine the beans, carrot, onion, celery, bouillon cubes, cumin, coriander, savory, chili powder, pepper, garlic, and the remaining 6 cups water. Stir to combine.

3. Cover; cook on low-heat setting for 12 to 14 hours or on high-heat setting for 6 to 7 hours. Mash beans slightly. Stir in half-and-half.

Nutrition Facts per serving: 346 calories, 6 g total fat, 15 mg cholesterol, 706 mg sodium, 56 g carbohydrate, 19 g protein.

1 pound dry black beans
   (about 2½ cups)
12 cups cold water
1 cup coarsely chopped carrot
1 cup coarsely chopped onion
1 cup coarsely chopped celery
2 vegetable
   bouillon cubes
2 teaspoons ground cumin
2 teaspoons ground coriander
2 teaspoons dried savory,
   crushed
1 teaspoon chili powder
½ teaspoon ground black
   pepper
2 cloves garlic, minced
1 cup half-and-half
   or light cream

Minestrone

Accompany this vegetable-rich soup with warm herbed bread sticks or focaccia.

Prep: 15 minutes **Cook:** 10 hours on low or 5 hours on high **Makes:** 8 servings

1 15-ounce can navy beans, rinsed and drained

1 cup shredded cabbage

½ cup sliced carrot

½ cup sliced celery

½ cup chopped onion

2 tablespoons fresh snipped parsley

1 clove garlic, minced

1 14½-ounce can tomatoes, undrained and cut up

1 10½-ounce can condensed beef broth

1½ teaspoons dried basil, crushed

¼ teaspoon dried oregano, crushed

3 cups water

¼ teaspoon ground black pepper

1 9-ounce package frozen Italian green beans

2 ounces dried spaghetti, broken into 1-inch pieces (½ cup)

Grated Parmesan cheese

1. In a 3½-, 4-, 5-, or 6-quart slow cooker place navy beans, cabbage, carrot, celery, onion, parsley, and garlic. Stir in undrained tomatoes, beef broth, basil, oregano, water, and pepper. Cover; cook on low-heat setting for 9 to 11 hours or on high-heat setting for 4 to 5 hours.

2. Rinse green beans under running water to separate. Stir green beans and spaghetti into soup mixture. Cover; cook on low-heat or high-heat setting for 1 hour more. Ladle into soup bowls. Sprinkle each serving with Parmesan cheese.

Nutrition Facts per serving: **155 calories, 2 g total fat, 4 mg cholesterol, 630 mg sodium, 25 g carbohydrate, 10 g protein.**

Winter Minestrone

Give this classic a pronounced Italian accent by using fresh escarole, a slightly bitter green that is much beloved by Southern Italians and widely available during the cold months.

Prep: 25 minutes **Cook:** 8 hours on low or 4 hours on high **Makes:** 8 servings

1. In a large skillet cook the sausage until brown; drain well.

2. In a 5- to 6-quart slow cooker place squash, potatoes, fennel, onion, garlic, beans, and sage. Top with sausage. Pour broth and wine over all.

3. Cover; cook on low-heat setting for 8 to 10 hours or on high-heat setting for 4 to 5 hours. Stir in kale. Cover; cook 5 minutes more.

Nutrition Facts per serving: 315 calories, 14 g total fat, 38 mg cholesterol, 933 mg sodium, 27 g carbohydrate, 16 g protein.

1 pound uncooked Italian
   or pork sausage links,
   cut into ¾-inch slices
2½ cups peeled winter squash,
   such as butternut squash,
   cut into 1-inch cubes
1½ cups cubed potatoes
2 medium fennel bulbs,
   trimmed and cut into
   1-inch pieces
1 large onion, chopped
2 cloves garlic, minced
1 15-ounce can red kidney
   beans, rinsed and drained
½ teaspoon dried sage, crushed
4 cups chicken broth
   or vegetable broth
1 cup dry white wine
4 cups chopped kale
   or fresh spinach
   or fresh escarole

Five-Bean Soup

With only one onion to chop, a hearty, delicious homemade soup doesn't get any easier than this one.

Prep: 15 minutes **Cook:** 10 hours on low or 5 hours on high **Makes:** 8 servings

1 15½-ounce can red kidney
   beans, rinsed and drained
1 15-ounce can garbanzo
   beans, rinsed and drained
1 15-ounce can navy beans,
   rinsed and drained
1 8½-ounce can lima beans,
   rinsed and drained
1 9-ounce package frozen
   cut green beans
1 cup chopped onion
1 4-ounce can diced green
   chile peppers, drained
4 teaspoons chili powder
1½ teaspoons dried basil,
   crushed
½ teaspoon dried oregano,
   crushed
¼ teaspoon bottled hot
   pepper sauce
2½ cups beef broth
1 12-ounce can beer
1 cup shredded cheddar
   cheese (4 ounces)

1. In a 3½-, 4-, 5-, or 6-quart slow cooker combine beans, green beans, onion, chile peppers, chili powder, basil, oregano, and hot pepper sauce. Stir in beef broth and beer.

2. Cover; cook on low-heat setting for 10 to 12 hours or on high-heat setting for 5 to 6 hours. Ladle into soup bowls. Top each serving with shredded cheese.

Nutrition Facts per serving: 301 calories, 6 g total fat, 15 mg cholesterol, 930 mg sodium, 44 g carbohydrate, 19 g protein.

Potato and Leek Soup

A package of frozen hash browns makes this creamy potato soup a no-peel proposition.

Prep: 15 minutes **Cook:** 7 hours on low plus 15 minutes on high or 3¾ hours on high **Makes:** 10 to 12 servings

1. In a 3½- or 4-quart slow cooker stir water into white sauce mix until mixture is smooth. Stir in potatoes, leeks, Canadian-style bacon, evaporated milk, and dillweed.

2. Cover; cook on low-heat setting for 7 to 9 hours or on high-heat setting for 3½ to 4½ hours.

3. If using low-heat setting, turn to high-heat setting. In a medium bowl stir about 2 cups of the hot potato mixture into the sour cream. Return sour cream mixture to cooker. Cover; cook about 15 minutes more on high-heat setting or until heated through. Ladle into bowls. If desired, sprinkle with parsley or additional sliced leek.

Nutrition Facts per serving: 212 calories, 10 g total fat, 28 mg cholesterol, 476 mg sodium, 23 g carbohydrate, 8 g protein.

3 cups water
1 1.8-ounce envelope white sauce mix
1 28-ounce package frozen loose-pack diced hash brown potatoes with onion and peppers
3 medium leeks, sliced (about 1 cup total)
1 cup diced Canadian-style bacon or cooked ham
1 12-ounce can evaporated milk
½ teaspoon dried dillweed
1 8-ounce carton dairy sour cream
Snipped fresh parsley or sliced leek (optional)

Southwest Vegetable Soup

Pump up the flavor of this soup with Mexican-style stewed tomatoes. Serve it with warm flour tortillas.

Prep: 15 minutes **Cook:** 7 hours on low or 3½ hours on high **Makes:** 6 to 8 servings

2 14½-ounce cans stewed
   tomatoes, undrained
1 15-ounce can black beans,
   rinsed and drained
1 cup chopped celery
1 cup water
1 8-ounce can whole kernel
   corn, drained
½ large green sweet pepper,
   chopped (¾ cup)
½ large onion, chopped
   (½ cup)
¼ cup dried vegetable soup
   mix
½ fresh jalapeño pepper,
   seeded and finely chopped
½ teaspoon dried cilantro,
   crushed
½ teaspoon garlic powder
½ teaspoon ground black
   pepper
¼ teaspoon dried basil,
   crushed
¼ teaspoon chili powder

In a 3½- or 4-quart slow cooker combine all ingredients. Cover; cook on low-heat setting for 7 to 8 hours or on high-heat setting for 3½ to 4 hours.

Nutrition Facts per serving: 209 calories, 2 g total fat, 0 mg cholesterol, 1,288 mg sodium, 44 g carbohydrate, 11 g protein.

Velvety Pumpkin Bisque

Creamy and elegant, this beautiful golden soup is just the thing to start off a holiday dinner in style.

Prep: 15 minutes **Cook:** 7 hours on low or 3½ hours on high **Makes:** 12 to 14 servings

1. In a 3½-, 4-, or 5-quart slow cooker combine pumpkin, chicken broth, onion, celery, brown sugar, pumpkin pie spice, salt, and pepper.

2. Cover; cook on low-heat setting for 7 to 8 hours or on high-heat setting for 3½ to 4 hours. Stir in half-and-half and butter.

Nutrition Facts per serving: **128 calories, 7 g total fat, 20 mg cholesterol, 402 mg sodium, 13 g carbohydrate, 4 g protein.**

3 15-ounce cans pumpkin
2 14-ounce cans chicken broth
½ cup finely chopped onion
½ cup finely chopped celery
2 tablespoons packed brown
 sugar
1 tablespoon pumpkin
 pie spice
¾ teaspoon salt
¼ teaspoon ground black
 pepper
2 cups half-and-half
 or light cream
2 tablespoons butter

Double-Bean Soup with Cornmeal Dumplings

You won't miss the meat in this chunky vegetable-bean soup that's topped with a crown of puffy, tender cornmeal dumplings.

Prep: 15 minutes **Cook:** 10½ hours on low **Makes:** 6 servings

3 cups water

1 15-ounce can red kidney beans, rinsed and drained

1 15-ounce can black beans, pinto beans, or Great Northern beans, rinsed and drained

1 14½-ounce can Mexican-style stewed tomatoes, undrained

1 10-ounce package frozen whole kernel corn

1 cup sliced carrot

1 cup chopped onion

1 4-ounce can diced green chile peppers, undrained

2 tablespoons instant beef or chicken bouillon granules

1 to 2 teaspoons chili powder

2 cloves garlic, minced

⅓ cup all-purpose flour

¼ cup yellow cornmeal

1 teaspoon baking powder

Dash salt

Dash ground black pepper

1 egg white, beaten

2 tablespoons milk

1 tablespoon cooking oil

1. In a 3½- or 4-quart slow cooker combine water, beans, tomatoes, corn, carrot, onion, chile peppers, bouillon granules, chili powder, and garlic. Cover; cook on low-heat setting for 10 to 12 hours.

2. In a medium mixing bowl stir together flour, cornmeal, baking powder, salt, and pepper. In a small mixing bowl combine egg white, milk, and oil. Add to flour mixture; stir with a fork just until combined. Drop dumpling mixture into 6 mounds on top of the bubbling soup. Cover; cook for 30 minutes more. (Do not lift lid while dumplings are cooking.)

Nutrition Facts per serving: 270 calories, 3 g total fat, 1 mg cholesterol, 1,593 mg sodium, 54 g carbohydrate, 15 g protein.

Potato-Cheese Soup

Mashing a few of the potatoes right before serving gives this popular spud soup great body.

Prep: 15 minutes **Cook:** 10 hours on low or 4½ hours on high **Makes:** 6 to 8 servings

---

1. In a 3½- or 4-quart slow cooker combine potatoes, water, onion, bouillon granules, and pepper. Cover; cook on low-heat setting for 9 to 11 hours or on high-heat setting 4 to 4½ hours.

2. Stir cheese and milk into soup. Cover; cook on low-heat setting for 1 hour more or on high-heat setting for 30 minutes more. Mash potatoes slightly.

For 5- or 6-quart slow cooker: Use 8 medium potatoes, peeled and chopped, 4 cups water, ¾ cup chopped onion, 1 tablespoon instant chicken bouillon granules, ¼ teaspoon pepper, 2 cups shredded American cheese (8 ounces), and one 12-ounce can evaporated milk plus one 5-ounce can evaporated milk. Prepare as above. Makes 9 to 12 servings.

Nutrition Facts per serving: **308 calories, 13 g total fat, 43 mg cholesterol, 765 mg sodium, 35 g carbohydrate, 14 g protein.**

6 medium potatoes, peeled and chopped (6 cups)
2½ cups water
½ cup chopped onion
2 teaspoons instant chicken bouillon granules
¼ teaspoon ground black pepper
1½ cups shredded American cheese (6 ounces)
1 12-ounce can evaporated milk (1½ cups)

Vegetarian Lentil Soup

Lentils are one of the few legumes that don't require long cooking times. Here, they simply benefit from it when combined with a medley of vegetables and seasonings.

Prep: 15 minutes **Cook:** 12 hours on low or 5 hours on high **Makes:** 6 servings

1 cup dry lentils
1 cup chopped carrot
1 cup chopped celery
1 cup chopped onion
2 cloves garlic, minced
½ teaspoon dried basil, crushed
½ teaspoon dried oregano, crushed
¼ teaspoon dried thyme, crushed
1 bay leaf
2 14-ounce cans vegetable broth or chicken broth
1½ cups water
1 14½-ounce can Italian-style stewed tomatoes, undrained
¼ cup snipped fresh parsley
2 tablespoons cider vinegar (optional)

1. Rinse lentils. In a 3½-, 4-, or 5-quart slow cooker place lentils, carrot, celery, onion, garlic, basil, oregano, thyme, and bay leaf. Stir in broth, water, and tomatoes.

2. Cover; cook on low-heat setting for 12 hours or on high-heat setting for 5 to 6 hours. Discard bay leaf. Stir in parsley and, if desired, vinegar.

Nutrition Facts per serving: **185 calories, 1 g total fat, 1 mg cholesterol, 725 mg sodium, 32 g carbohydrate, 13 g protein.**

Cheesy Vegetable Soup

Even kids will eat their veggies when they come cloaked in a creamy, cheesy bowlful of soup. Serve it with fresh fruit and corn bread.

Prep: 15 minutes **Cook:** 10½ hours on low plus 30 minutes on high or 4½ hours on high **Makes:** 4 servings

1. In a 3½-, 4-, or 5-quart slow cooker combine corn, potatoes, carrot, onion, celery seeds, and pepper. Add broth.

2. Cover; cook on low-heat setting for 10 to 11 hours or on high-heat setting for 4 to 4½ hours.

3. If using low-heat setting, turn to high-heat setting. Stir cheese into hot soup. Cover; cook on high-heat setting 30 to 60 minutes longer or until cheese is melted.

Nutrition Facts per serving: **291 calories, 11 g total fat, 25 mg cholesterol, 1,575 mg sodium, 38 g carbohydrate, 14 g protein.**

1 16½-ounce can cream-style corn
1 cup chopped, peeled potatoes
½ cup shredded carrot
½ cup chopped onion
½ teaspoon celery seeds
¼ teaspoon ground black pepper
2 14-ounce cans vegetable broth or chicken broth
1½ cups shredded American cheese (6 ounces)

Vegetable Barley Soup

Light and fresh, this soup is terrific when paired with a sandwich for a healthful and satisfying lunch.

Prep: 20 minutes **Cook:** 9 hours on low or 4½ hours on high **Makes:** 5 servings

3 cups water

1 14½-ounce can diced tomatoes, undrained

1 10-oz. package frozen mixed vegetables

1 medium zucchini, quartered lengthwise and sliced (2 cups)

2 stalks celery, chopped (1 cup)

2 medium carrots, chopped (1 cup)

1 medium onion, chopped (½ cup)

½ of an 8-ounce can tomato sauce (about ½ cup)

⅓ cup regular barley

2 vegetable bouillon cubes or 4 teaspoons instant chicken bouillon granules

½ teaspoon dried basil, crushed

¼ teaspoon dried oregano, crushed

Dash ground red pepper

1. In a 3½- or 4-quart slow cooker combine all ingredients. Cover; cook on low-heat setting for 9 to 11 hours or cook on high-heat setting for 4½ to 5½ hours.

Nutrition Facts per serving: 134 calories, 1 g total fat, 0 mg cholesterol, 702 mg sodium, 29 g carbohydrate, 5 g protein.

Savory Spinach Soup

Stirring the fresh spinach in right before serving ensures that it will be tender, flavorful, and a beautiful bright green color that's enticing to eat.

Prep: 15 minutes **Cook:** 5 hours on low or 2½ hours on high **Makes:** 6 servings

1. In a 3½- or 4-quart slow cooker place onion, garlic, tomato puree, drained beans, rice, vegetable broth, basil, salt, and pepper.

2. Cover; cook on low-heat setting for 5 to 7 hours or on high-heat setting for 2½ to 3½ hours. Stir in spinach. To serve, ladle into bowls and top with Parmesan cheese.

Nutrition Facts per serving: **150 calories, 3 g total fat, 4 mg cholesterol, 1,137 mg sodium, 31 g carbohydrate, 9 g protein.**

½ cup finely chopped onion
2 cloves garlic, minced
1 15-ounce can tomato puree
1 15-ounce can white or
   Great Northern beans,
   rinsed and drained
½ cup uncooked long grain rice
3 14-ounce cans vegetable
   broth
1 teaspoon dried basil, crushed
¼ teaspoon salt
¼ teaspoon ground black
   pepper
8 cups coarsely chopped fresh
   spinach or kale leaves
   (about 8 ounces)
   Finely shredded Parmesan
   cheese

Spicy Pumpkin Soup

Put this warming soup on to simmer on a chilly autumn day. Top it with crunchy pumpkin seeds (pepitas), which can be found in large supermarkets, health foods stores, or Hispanic markets.

Prep: 10 minutes **Cook:** 6 hours on low or 3 hours on high **Makes:** 6 to 8 servings

---

1 16-ounce can pumpkin

1 cup chopped celery

½ cup chopped carrot

½ cup chopped onion

½ teaspoon salt

½ teaspoon dried oregano, crushed

½ teaspoon dried rosemary, crushed

¼ teaspoon ground red pepper

4 cups vegetable broth or chicken broth

2 medium tomatoes, peeled and chopped, or one 8-ounce can tomatoes, undrained and cut up

Dairy sour cream or plain yogurt (optional)

Shelled pumpkin or sunflower seeds (optional)

1. In a 3½- or 4-quart slow cooker place pumpkin, celery, carrot, onion, salt, oregano, rosemary, and red pepper. Gradually stir in broth.

2. Cover; cook on low-heat setting for 6 to 8 hours or on high-heat setting for 3 to 4 hours. Stir in tomatoes. Ladle into bowls. If desired, add a tablespoon of sour cream and sprinkle with seeds.

Nutrition Facts per serving: 56 calories, 1 g total fat, 0 mg cholesterol, 918 mg sodium, 15 g carbohydrate, 2 g protein.

Dilled Barley Vegetable Soup

Dill gives this soup a taste of summer. Serve it with drop biscuits, and for dessert serve frozen yogurt.

Prep: 10 minutes   **Cook:** 8 hours on low or 4 hours on high   **Makes:** 6 servings

1. In a 3½-, 4-, or 5-quart slow cooker place beans, corn, barley, tomatoes, mushrooms, onion, carrot, celery, garlic, dillweed, pepper, and bay leaf. Pour broth over all.

2. Cover; cook on low-heat setting for 8 to 10 hours or on high-heat setting for 4 to 5 hours.

3. Discard bay leaf.

Nutrition Facts per serving: **191 calories, 2 g total fat, 0 mg cholesterol, 1,111 mg sodium, 45 g carbohydrate, 10 g protein.**

1 15-ounce can red beans, rinsed and drained
1 10-ounce package frozen whole kernel corn
½ cup medium pearl barley
1 14½-ounce can stewed tomatoes, undrained
2 cups sliced fresh mushrooms
1 cup chopped onion
1 medium carrot, coarsely chopped (½ cup)
1 stalk celery, coarsely chopped (½ cup)
3 cloves garlic, minced
2 teaspoons dried dillweed
¼ teaspoon ground black pepper
1 bay leaf
5 cups vegetable broth or chicken broth

Creamy Clam Chowder

Can't keep your chowders straight? This creamy bacon-topped version is the one that's usually referred to as New-England style.

Prep: 20 minutes **Cook:** 8 hours on low plus 15 minutes on high or 4¼ hours on high **Makes:** 6 to 8 servings

2 6½-ounce cans minced clams

2 cups peeled potatoes, cut into ½-inch cubes

1 cup finely chopped onion

1 cup chopped celery

½ cup shredded carrot

1 teaspoon sugar

¼ teaspoon salt

¼ teaspoon ground black pepper

2 10¾-ounce cans condensed cream of potato soup

3 cups water

1 cup nonfat dry milk powder

⅓ cup all-purpose flour

4 slices bacon, crisp-cooked, drained, and crumbled Paprika

1. Drain clams, reserving liquid. Cover clams; chill.

2. In a 3½-, 4-, or 5-quart slow cooker combine reserved clam liquid, potatoes, onion, celery, carrot, sugar, salt, and pepper. Stir in potato soup and 2 cups of the water.

3. Cover; cook on low-heat setting for 8 to 10 hours or on high-heat setting for 4 to 5 hours.

4. If using low-heat setting, turn to high-heat setting. In a medium bowl combine milk powder and flour. Gradually whisk in the remaining 1 cup cold water; stir into soup. Cover; cook on high-heat setting 10 to 15 minutes or until thickened.

5. Stir in clams. Cover; cook 5 minutes more. Ladle soup into bowls. Sprinkle each serving with crumbled bacon and paprika.

Nutrition Facts per serving: 268 calories, 5 g total fat, 49 mg cholesterol, 735 mg sodium, 43 g carbohydrate, 14 g protein.

Manhattan Clam Chowder

It turns out saving time is good for you: Don't peel the nutrient-rich potatoes.

Simply scrub the skins well, then cut the potatoes into cubes.

Prep: 15 minutes **Cook:** 8 hours on low plus 5 minutes on high or 4 hours on high **Makes:** 6 servings

1. Drain clams, reserving liquid. Cover clams; chill.

2. In a 3½- or 4-quart slow cooker combine reserved clam liquid, potatoes, onion, celery, sweet pepper, tomatoes, tomato juice, salt, thyme, and bay leaf.

3. Cover; cook on low-heat setting for 8 to 10 hours or on high-heat setting for 4 to 5 hours.

4. If using low-heat setting, turn to high-heat setting. Stir in clams. Cover; cook on high-heat setting 5 minutes. Discard bay leaf. Ladle soup into bowls. Sprinkle each serving with crumbled bacon.

Nutrition Facts per serving: 146 calories, 3 g total fat, 42 mg cholesterol, 761 mg sodium, 24 g carbohydrate, 9 g protein.

- 2 6½-ounce cans minced clams
- 2 cups potatoes, cut into ½-inch cubes
- 1 cup chopped onion
- 1 cup chopped celery with leaves
- ½ cup chopped green sweet pepper
- 1 14½-ounce can Italian-style stewed tomatoes, undrained
- 1½ cups hot-style tomato juice or hot-style vegetable juice
- ½ teaspoon salt
- ½ teaspoon dried thyme, crushed
- 1 bay leaf
- 4 slices bacon, crisp-cooked, drained, and crumbled

Corn and Sausage Chowder

A fresh chive garnish adds color and a little something extra to this sunny golden soup.

Prep: 10 minutes **Cook:** 8 hours on low or 4 hours on high **Makes:** 6 servings

1 pound fully cooked smoked
   turkey sausage, halved
   lengthwise and cut into
   ½-inch slices
3 cups loose-pack frozen hash
   brown potatoes with onions
   and peppers
1 medium carrot, coarsely
   chopped (½ cup)
1 stalk celery, coarsely
   chopped (½ cup)
2 10¾-ounce cans condensed
   golden corn soup
2½ cups water
   Snipped fresh chives
   or fresh parsley

1. In a 3½-, 4-, or 5-quart slow cooker place sausage, hash brown potatoes, carrot, and celery. In a bowl combine soup and water. Add to cooker.

2. Cover; cook on low-heat setting for 8 to 10 hours or on high-heat setting for 4 to 5 hours. Ladle into bowls. Sprinkle with chives.

Nutrition Facts per serving: 275 calories, 8 g total fat, 52 mg cholesterol, 668 mg sodium, 32 g carbohydrate, 16 g protein.

Brunswick Fish Chowder

Although it's not recommended that frozen meat or poultry be used in the slow cooker, using partially frozen fish keeps the delicate flesh from overcooking.

Prep: 20 minutes **Cook:** 7 hours on low or 3½ hours on high **Makes:** 6 servings

1. Let fish stand at room temperature while preparing all of the other ingredients.

2. In a 3½-, 4-, or 5-quart slow cooker combine potatoes, onion, garlic, soup, corn, lima beans, chicken broth, white wine, lemon-pepper seasoning, and bay leaf. Halve the fillets crosswise; place frozen fish fillet halves in the cooker.

3. Cover; cook on low-heat setting for 7 to 8 hours or on high-heat setting for 3½ to 4 hours.

4. Discard bay leaf. Break fish into bite-size chunks with a fork. Stir in undrained tomatoes and dry milk powder.

Nutrition Facts per serving: 300 calories, 4 g total fat, 37 mg cholesterol, 1,058 mg sodium, 44 g carbohydrate, 23 g protein.

1 pound frozen cod
   or whiting fillets
2 medium potatoes,
   finely chopped
1 cup chopped onion
2 cloves garlic, minced
1 10¾-ounce can condensed
   cream of celery soup
1 10-ounce package frozen
   whole kernel corn
1 10-ounce package frozen
   baby lima beans
1½ cups chicken broth
⅓ cup dry white wine or water
1 teaspoon lemon-pepper
   seasoning
1 bay leaf
1 14½-ounce can stewed
   tomatoes, undrained
⅓ cup nonfat dry milk powder

Mexican Chicken Chowder

Stirring a little hot soup into the sour cream before adding it to the big pot keeps it from curdling.

Prep: 15 minutes **Cook:** 8 hours on low or 4 hours on high **Stand:** 5 minutes **Makes:** 6 servings

2½ **cups chopped cooked chicken**

1 **11-ounce can whole kernel corn with sweet peppers, drained**

1 **10¾-ounce can condensed cream of potato soup**

1 **4-ounce can diced green chile peppers, undrained**

2 **tablespoons snipped fresh cilantro**

1 **1¼-ounce envelope taco seasoning mix**

3 **cups chicken broth**

1 **8-ounce carton dairy sour cream**

½ **of an 8-ounce package cheese spread with jalapeño peppers**

1. In a 3½- or 4-quart slow cooker combine chicken, corn, soup, chile peppers, cilantro, and taco seasoning mix. Stir in chicken broth.

2. Cover; cook on low-heat setting for 8 to 10 hours or on high-heat setting for 4 to 5 hours.

3. Stir about 1 cup of the hot soup into sour cream. Stir sour cream mixture and cheese into the mixture in slow cooker; cover and let stand 5 minutes. Stir until combined.

Nutrition Facts per serving: 351 calories, 20 g total fat, 80 mg cholesterol, 1,986 mg sodium, 20 g carbohydrate, 26 g protein.

Classic Chili

Have some friends over to watch the big game—and enjoy a hearty bowl of chili slowly simmered in an unwatched pot, allowing you to play host rather than kitchen crew.

Prep: 20 minutes **Cook:** 8 hours on low or 4 hours on high **Makes:** 4 servings

1. In a large saucepan cook ground beef, onion, sweet pepper, and garlic until meat is brown and onion is tender. Drain fat.

2. In a 3½- or 4-quart slow cooker combine meat mixture, tomatoes, beans, tomato sauce, chili powder, basil, and pepper. Cover; cook on low-heat setting for 8 to 10 hours on high-heat setting for 4 to 5 hours.

Nutrition Facts per serving: **308 calories, 11 g total fat, 53 mg cholesterol, 755 mg sodium, 31 g carbohydrate, 26 g protein.**

12 ounces ground beef

 1 cup chopped onion (1 large)

 ½ cup chopped green
   sweet pepper

 2 cloves garlic, minced

 1 14½-ounce can tomatoes,
   undrained and cut up

 1 15-ounce can dark red kidney
   beans, rinsed and drained

 1 8-ounce can tomato sauce

 2 to 3 teaspoons chili powder

 ½ teaspoon dried basil, crushed

 ¼ teaspoon ground black
   pepper

Old-Fashioned Beef Stew

Beef and vegetables in a rich broth make this a perennial favorite.

Prep: 25 minutes **Cook:** 10 hours on low or 5 hours on high **Makes:** 4 to 6 servings

2 tablespoons all-purpose flour
1 pound beef or pork
    stew meat, cut into
    ¾-inch cubes
2 tablespoons cooking oil
2½ cups cubed potatoes
1 cup frozen cut green beans
1 cup frozen whole kernel corn
1 cup sliced carrot
1 medium onion, cut into
    thin wedges
2 teaspoons instant beef
    bouillon granules
2 teaspoons Worcestershire
    sauce
1 teaspoon dried oregano,
    crushed
½ teaspoon dried marjoram
    or basil, crushed
¼ teaspoon ground black
    pepper
1 bay leaf
2½ cups vegetable juice or
    hot-style vegetable juice

1. Place flour in a plastic bag. Add meat cubes and shake until meat is coated with flour. In a large skillet brown half of the meat in 1 tablespoon of the hot 1 tablespoon hot oil, turning to brown evenly. Brown remaining meat in remaining oil. Drain off fat.

2. In a 3½- or 4-quart slow cooker layer potatoes, green beans, corn, carrot, and onion. Add meat. Add bouillon granules, Worcestershire sauce, oregano, marjoram, pepper, and bay leaf. Pour vegetable juice over all.

3. Cover; cook on low-heat setting for 10 to 12 hours or on high-heat setting for 5 to 6 hours or until meat and vegetables are tender. Discard bay leaf.

Nutrition Facts per serving: 525 calories, 28 g total fat, 77 mg cholesterol, 953 mg sodium, 42 g carbohydrate, 27 g protein.

Beef and Fresh Mushroom Stew

A mushroom medley makes this sherried soup extra special. Be sure to remove and discard the tough stems before slicing the caps of shiitake mushrooms.

Prep: 20 minutes **Cook:** 8 hours on low or 4 hours on high **Makes:** 6 servings

1. In a 4-, 5-, or 6-quart slow cooker place mushrooms, carrots, celery, and rice mix with seasoning packet. Place meat on top of vegetables. Pour broth and sherry over all.

2. Cover; cook on low-heat setting for 8 to 10 hours or on high-heat setting for 4 to 5 hours.

Nutrition Facts per serving: 279 calories, 5 g total fat, 43 mg cholesterol, 1,394 mg sodium, 30 g carbohydrate, 24 g protein.

4 cups sliced assorted fresh
   mushrooms, such as button,
   crimini, and shiitake
3 medium carrots, cut into
   ½-inch slices (1½ cups)
1 cup sliced celery
1 6-ounce package long grain
   and wild rice mix
1 pound beef stew meat,
   cut into 1-inch cubes
6 cups beef broth
½ cup dry sherry

Tex-Mex Chili

If you like your chili hot, add a minced jalapeño or two and use hot-style vegetable juice.

Prep: 15 minutes **Cook:** 8 hours on low or 4 hours on high **Makes:** 4 to 6 servings

1 pound ground beef
   or bulk pork sausage
2 cloves garlic, minced
3 to 4 teaspoons chili powder
½ teaspoon ground cumin
1 15½-ounce can red kidney
   beans, rinsed and drained
1 cup chopped celery
1 cup chopped onion
½ cup chopped green
   sweet pepper
1 16-ounce can tomatoes,
   undrained and cut up
1 10-ounce can tomatoes
   with green chile peppers,
   undrained
1 cup vegetable juice
   or tomato juice
1 6-ounce can tomato paste
¼ teaspoon salt
   Shredded cheddar cheese
   Dairy sour cream

1. In a large skillet cook the beef and garlic until meat is brown. Drain off fat. Stir in chili powder and cumin; cook 2 minutes more.

2. Meanwhile, in a 3½-, 4-, or 5-quart slow cooker combine beans, celery, onion, and sweet pepper. Add tomatoes, tomatoes with chile peppers, vegetable juice, tomato paste, and salt. Stir in meat mixture.

3. Cover; cook on low-heat setting for 8 to 10 hours or on high-heat setting for 4 to 5 hours. Ladle chili into soup bowls. Pass shredded cheese and sour cream with chili.

Nutrition Facts per serving: 477 calories, 25 g total fat, 66 mg cholesterol, 2,012 mg sodium, 44 g carbohydrate, 26 g protein.

Salsa Verde Beef Stew

A salad of romaine, orange sections, and avocado slices drizzled with a cumin vinaigrette would be a fresh accompaniment to this hearty stew.

Prep: 30 minutes   **Cook:** 8 hours on low or 5 hours on high   **Makes:** 6 servings

1. Trim fat from meat. Cut beef into 1-inch pieces. In a large skillet brown half of the beef at a time in hot oil over medium-high heat.

2. In a 3½-, 4-, or 5-quart slow cooker combine beef, potatoes, onion, sweet pepper, tomatoes, beans, salsa, garlic and cumin. Cover; cook on low-heat setting for 8 to 9 hours or on high-heat setting for 5 to 6 hours. Serve with warmed tortillas.

Nutrition Facts per serving: 465 calories, 12 g total fat, 72 mg cholesterol, 709 mg sodium, 56 g carbohydrate, 33 g protein.

1½ pounds boneless beef
 chuck pot roast
1 tablespoon cooking oil
4 medium unpeeled potatoes,
 cut into 1-inch pieces
1 large onion, coarsely
 chopped (1 cup)
1 green sweet pepper,
 cut into ½-inch pieces
 (¾ cup)
1 14½-ounce can Mexican-
 style stewed tomatoes,
 undrained (¾ cup)
1 15- or 16-ounce can pinto
 beans, rinsed and drained
1 cup bottled mild or medium
 green salsa
2 cloves garlic, minced
1 teaspoon ground cumin
6 flour tortillas

Meatball and Vegetable Stew

Keep the ingredients for this easy stew on hand. Even as late as 4 p.m. you'll never need

to ask yourself what you're having for dinner!

Prep: 10 minutes **Cook:** 6 hours on low or 3 hours on high **Makes:** 4 servings

1 16- to 18-ounce package
    frozen cooked meatballs

½ of a 16-ounce package
    frozen mixed vegetables
    (about 2 cups)

1 14½-ounce can diced
    tomatoes with onion and
    garlic, or stewed tomatoes;
    undrained

1 12-ounce jar mushroom
    gravy

1½ teaspoons dried basil,
    crushed

⅓ cup water

1. In a 3½- or 4-quart slow cooker place meatballs and mixed vegetables. In a bowl stir together tomatoes, gravy, basil, and ⅓ cup water; pour over meatballs and vegetables.

2. Cover; cook on low-heat setting for 6 to 8 hours or on high-heat setting for 3 to 4 hours.

Nutrition Facts per serving: 472 calories, 32 g total fat, 87 mg cholesterol, 1,883 mg sodium, 26 g carbohydrate, 21 g protein.

Provençal Beef Stew

Herbes de Provence (a blend of basil, fennel, lavender, marjoram, rosemary, sage, savory, and thyme), red wine, and olives add a French touch to this dish.

Prep: 20 minutes **Cook:** 10 hours on low or 4 hours on high **Makes:** 6 servings

1. Peel a strip from the center of each potato. Place potatoes, carrots, shallots, and olives in a 4-quart slow cooker; top with beef. Combine broth, garlic, herbes de Provence, salt, pepper, and tapioca; pour over beef.

2. Cover; cook on low-heat setting for 10 to 12 hours or on high-heat setting for 4 to 5 hours. Stir in wine during last 30 minutes of cooking. If desired, sprinkle with parsley and garnish with capers.

Nutrition Facts per serving: **198 calories, 5 g total fat, 54 mg cholesterol, 308 mg sodium, 16 g carbohydrate, 20 g protein.**

8 small new potatoes
1 pound small carrots with tops, peeled and trimmed, or one 1-pound package peeled baby carrots
1 cup cut-up, peeled shallots or coarsely chopped onion
½ cup green and/or black European-style olives, pitted
1½ pounds lean boneless beef chuck roast, cut into 2-inch pieces
1 cup beef broth
4 to 6 cloves garlic, minced
1 teaspoon herbes de Provence
¼ teaspoon salt
¼ teaspoon whole black pepper or cracked black pepper
1 tablespoon quick-cooking tapioca
¼ cup dry red wine
Snipped fresh parsley (optional)
Capers (optional)

Santa Fe Beef Stew

If you can't find jalapeño pinto beans, add one finely chopped jalapeño pepper to the mix.

Prep: 25 minutes **Cook:** 10 hours on low plus 30 minutes on high or 5½ hours on high **Makes:** 6 servings

1 pound beef chuck pot roast

1 tablespoon cooking oil

2 14½-ounce cans Mexican-style stewed tomatoes, undrained

1½ cups coarsely chopped onion

1 15-ounce can pinto beans or jalapeño pinto beans, rinsed and drained

3½ cups beef broth

1 6-ounce can tomato paste

4 teaspoons chili powder

1 tablespoon dried Italian seasoning, crushed

½ teaspoon crushed red pepper

¼ teaspoon ground cloves

¼ teaspoon ground allspice

¼ teaspoon ground cinnamon

1 medium zucchini, halved lengthwise, and cut into ½-inch pieces (2 cups)

1 medium yellow or green sweet pepper, cut into 1-inch pieces (¾ cups)

1. Trim fat from meat. Cut meat into 1-inch cubes. In a large skillet brown meat, half at a time, in hot oil. Drain off fat.

2. Transfer meat to a 3½-, 4-, or 5-quart slow cooker. Add tomatoes, onion, and beans.

3. In a bowl combine beef broth, tomato paste, chili powder, Italian seasoning, red pepper, cloves, allspice, and cinnamon. Add to meat mixture in cooker.

4. Cover; cook on low-heat setting for 10 to 12 hours or on high-heat setting for 5 to 6 hours.

5. If using low-heat setting, turn to high-heat setting. Add zucchini and sweet pepper. Cover; cook 30 minutes longer on high-heat setting.

Nutrition Facts per serving: 360 calories, 10 g total fat, 76 mg cholesterol, 1,258 mg sodium, 35 g carbohydrate, 35 g protein.

Kielbasa Stew

Try to use reduced-sodium chicken broth, if you can; the sausage adds plenty of salt to this stew.

Prep: 20 minutes **Cook:** 7 hours on low or 3½ hours on high **Makes:** 4 or 5 servings

1. In a 4- or 5-quart slow cooker combine cabbage, potato, and carrot. Top with kielbasa. Sprinkle basil, thyme, and pepper over kielbasa. Pour chicken broth over all.

2. Cover; cook on low-heat setting for 7 to 9 hours or on high-heat setting for 3½ to 4½ hours.

Nutrition Facts per serving: 522 calories, 34 g total fat, 76 mg cholesterol, 1,658 mg sodium, 34 g carbohydrate, 23 g protein.

4 cups coarsely chopped
  cabbage
3 cups peeled, cubed potato
1½ cups sliced carrot
1 pound cooked kielbasa
  (Polska kielbasa), sliced
½ teaspoon dried basil, crushed
½ teaspoon dried thyme,
  crushed
½ teaspoon ground black
  pepper
2 14-ounce cans reduced-
  sodium chicken broth

Pork and Hominy Stew

In Mexico, the combination of pork, hominy, and chili powder in a savory broth has a special name—posole—and people have been known to close shop early on the day it's the special at the local cafe.

Prep: 25 minutes **Cook:** 8 hours on low or 4 hours on high **Makes:** 6 servings

---

1 pound boneless
   pork shoulder
1 tablespoon cooking oil
1 medium red or green
   sweet pepper, cut into
   ½-inch pieces (¾ cup)
1 medium tomato, chopped
½ cup chopped onion
4 cloves garlic, minced
2 16-ounce cans golden
   hominy, drained
1 4-ounce can diced green
   chile peppers, drained
1 tablespoon chili powder
½ teaspoon dried oregano,
   crushed
2 14-ounce cans
   chicken broth
   Tortilla chips (optional)

1. Trim fat from meat; cut pork into 1-inch cubes. In a large skillet brown pork, half at a time, in hot oil. Drain off fat.

2. Transfer pork to a 3½-, 4-, or 5-quart slow cooker. Add sweet pepper, tomato, onion, garlic, hominy, chile peppers, chili powder, and oregano. Pour broth over all.

3. Cover; cook on low-heat setting for 8 to 10 hours or on high-heat setting for 4 to 5 hours. If Desired, serve with tortilla chips.

Nutrition Facts per serving: **289 calories, 11 g total fat, 50 mg cholesterol, 897 mg sodium, 27 g carbohydrate, 19 g protein.**

Italian Pork and Bean Stew

A little bit of pork sausage gives this stew great flavor. You can also use ground turkey that's spiced to taste like Italian pork sausage.

Prep: 30 minutes **Stand:** 1 hour **Cook:** 7 hours on low plus 15 minutes on high or 3¾ hours on high **Makes:** 6 servings

1. Rinse beans; drain. In a large saucepan combine beans and 6 cups of the water. Bring to boiling; reduce heat. Simmer, uncovered, for 10 minutes. Remove from heat. Cover and let stand for 1 hour. Drain and rinse beans. Transfer beans to a 3½-, 4-, or 5-quart slow cooker; add carrot.

2. In a large skillet cook sausage, onion, and garlic over medium heat until sausage is no longer pink, breaking up sausage as it cooks. Drain off fat. Transfer mixture to slow cooker. Add cubed pork.

3. Stir in the remaining 3 cups water, bouillon granules, thyme, and oregano. Cover; cook on low-heat setting for 7 to 8 hours or on high-heat setting for 3½ to 4 hours.

4. If using low-heat setting, turn to high-heat setting. Stir wine into tomato paste. Add to mixture in cooker along with parsley. Cover; cook for 15 minutes more.

Nutrition Facts per serving: 473 calories, 13 g total fat, 73 mg cholesterol, 566 mg sodium, 49 g carbohydrate, 37 g protein.

- **2 cups dry Great Northern beans**
- **9 cups cold water**
- **1½ cups carrot, cut into ½-inch pieces**
- **8 ounces bulk Italian sausage**
- **1½ cups coarsely chopped onion**
- **3 cloves garlic, minced**
- **1 pound lean boneless pork, cut into cubes**
- **1 teaspoon instant beef bouillon granules**
- **½ teaspoon dried thyme, crushed**
- **½ teaspoon dried oregano, crushed**
- **¼ cup dry red wine**
- **⅓ cup tomato paste (½ of a 6-ounce can)**
- **¼ cup snipped fresh parsley**

Sweet Potato and Sausage Stew

Tapioca added to slow-cooked stews such as this one thickens them without making them pasty.

Prep: 15 minutes **Cook:** 10 hours on low or 4½ hours on high **Makes:** 4 servings

1 pound smoked turkey
   sausage links
2 small sweet potatoes,
   peeled and cut into
   ½-inch pieces (2 cups)
1 medium sweet green pepper,
   cut into 1-inch pieces
   (¾ cup)
1 stalk celery, cut into
   ½-inch pieces (½ cup)
½ cup chopped onion
2 tablespoons quick-cooking
   tapioca
1 14½-ounce can tomatoes,
   undrained and cut up
1 15-ounce can garbanzo
   beans, rinsed and drained
1 cup beef broth

1. Cut sausage in half lengthwise; cut into 1-inch slices.

In a 3½, 4-, 5-, or 6-quart slow cooker combine sausage pieces, sweet potatoes, pepper, celery, onion, and tapioca. Add tomatoes, garbanzo beans, and beef broth.

2. Cover; cook on low-heat setting for 10 to 12 hours or on high-heat setting for 4½ to 5 hours.

Nutrition Facts per serving: 438 calories, 11 g total fat, 76 mg cholesterol, 1,800 mg sodium, 57 g carbohydrate, 29 g protein.

Lone Star Stew

All over the South, black-eyed peas are standard good-luck fare for New Year's Day.
Revel in the tradition with this Southwest-style take on the dish.

Prep: 20 minutes **Cook:** 8 hours on low plus 30 minutes on high or 4½ hours on high **Makes:** 6 servings

1. Sort through peas to remove any pebbles or other foreign matter. Rinse peas; combine with 5 cups of the water in a large saucepan. Bring to boiling; reduce heat. Cook, uncovered, over low heat for 10 minutes. Drain and rinse.

2. In a 4- or 4½-quart slow cooker combine peas, the quartered jalapeños, sage, salt, and the remaining 3 cups water. Add turkey.

3. Cover; cook on low-heat setting for 8 to 10 hours or on high-heat setting for 4 to 5 hours. If using low-heat setting, turn to high-heat setting.

4. Stir in squash; cover; cook 30 minutes more. Serve topped with red onion, cilantro, and, if desired, Lime Sour Cream and chopped jalapeño pepper.

Nutrition Facts per serving: **144 calories, 1 g total fat, 47 mg cholesterol, 423 mg sodium, 13 g carbohydrate, 21 g protein.**

Lime Sour Cream: Combine ½ cup light dairy sour cream, ½ teaspoon finely shredded lime peel, and 1 teaspoon lime juice in a small bowl. Cover and chill before serving.

- 2 cups dry black-eyed peas (12 ounce)
- 8 cups water
- 1 to 3 whole jalapeño peppers, quartered lengthwise
- 1½ teaspoons dried sage, crushed
- 1 teaspoon salt
- 1 pound turkey or pork tenderloin, cut into 1½-inch pieces
- 2 medium yellow summer squashes, cut into wedges (about 2½ cups)
- ½ cup finely chopped red onion
- Snipped fresh cilantro
- Lime Sour Cream (optional)
- Finely chopped jalapeño pepper (optional)

Pork Stew with Cornmeal Dumplings

If you're rushed and don't have time to make the cornmeal dumplings, serve the stew with cornmeal muffins or corn bread.

Prep: 25 minutes **Cook:** 9 hours on low plus 50 minutes on high or 4 hours 50 minutes on high **Makes:** 4 servings

---

1 1-pound boneless pork
   shoulder roast
1 clove garlic, minced
1 tablespoon cooking oil
4 medium carrots, cut into
   ½-inch pieces (2 cups)
2 medium potatoes, peeled
   and cubed (2 cups)
1 12-ounce can beer
¼ cup quick-cooking tapioca
1 tablespoon sugar
1 tablespoon Worcestershire
   sauce
2 bay leaves
1 teaspoon dried thyme,
   crushed
½ teaspoon salt
¼ teaspoon ground nutmeg
¼ teaspoon ground black
   pepper
1 28-ounce can tomatoes,
   undrained and cut up
   Cornmeal Dumplings
2 tablespoons shredded
   cheddar cheese

1. Trim fat from pork. Cut pork into 1-inch cubes. In a large skillet brown pork and garlic in hot oil. Drain well.

2. Meanwhile, in a 3½- or 4-quart slow cooker combine carrots, potatoes, beer, tapioca, sugar, Worcestershire sauce, bay leaves, thyme, salt, nutmeg, and pepper. Stir in browned meat and tomatoes. Cover; cook on low-heat setting for 9 to 11 hours or on high-heat setting for 4 to 5 hours.

3. If using low-heat setting, turn to high-heat setting. Prepare Cornmeal Dumplings. Remove bay leaves. Stir stew; drop dumplings by tablespoonfuls onto stew. Cover; cook for 50 minutes more (do not lift cover). Sprinkle dumplings with cheese.

Cornmeal Dumplings

½ cup all-purpose flour	Dash ground black pepper
½ cup shredded cheddar cheese	1 egg, beaten
⅓ cup yellow cornmeal	2 tablespoons milk
1 teaspoon baking powder	2 tablespoons cooking oil

In a medium mixing bowl stir together flour, cheese, cornmeal, baking powder, and pepper. Combine egg, milk, and oil. Add to flour mixture; stir with a fork just until combined.

For 5- or 6-quart slow cooker: Use one 1½-pound boneless pork shoulder roast, 5 medium carrots, and 3 medium potatoes. Leave remaining ingredient amounts the same. Makes 6 servings.

Nutrition Facts per serving: 649 calories, 25 g total fat, 146 mg cholesterol, 980 mg sodium, 65 g carbohydrate, 36 g protein.

Green Chile Stew

Hominy—dried white or yellow corn from which the hull has been removed—adds a pleasantly chewy texture to this Tex-Mex style stew.

Prep: 25 minutes **Cook:** 7 hours on low or 4 hours on high **Makes:** 5 to 6 servings

1. Trim fat from pork. Cut pork into ½-inch cubes. In a large skillet brown half of the pork in hot oil. Transfer meat to a 3½- or 4 ½-quart slow cooker. Brown remaining meat with onion. Drain off the fat and transfer meat and onion to the slow cooker.

2. Add water, potatoes, hominy, chile peppers, tapioca, garlic salt, salt, black pepper, cumin, and oregano. Cover; cook on low-heat setting for 7 to 8 hours or on high-heat setting for 4 to 5 hours. If desired, garnish with snipped cilantro.

Nutrition Facts per serving: 414 calories, 11 g total fat, 102 mg cholesterol, 980 mg sodium, 40 g carbohydrate, 39 g protein.

2 pounds boneless pork sirloin
    or shoulder roast
1 tablespoon cooking oil
½ cup chopped onion
3 cups water
4 medium potatoes, peeled
    and cut into ½-inch cubes
    (4 cups)
1 15-ounce can hominy or
    whole kernel corn, drained
2 4-ounce cans chopped
    green chile peppers, drained
2 tablespoons quick-cooking
    tapioca
1 teaspoon garlic salt
½ teaspoon salt
½ teaspoon ground
    black pepper
½ teaspoon ground cumin
⅛ teaspoon dried oregano,
    crushed
    Snipped fresh cilantro
    (optional)

Persian-Style Stew

As the yellow split peas simmer, they fall apart and give the stew a thick, hearty consistency. The small amount of raisins provides a slight sweetness.

Prep: 25 minutes **Cook:** 8 hours on low plus 15 minutes on high or 4¼ hours on high **Makes:** 6 to 8 servings

1½ to 2 pounds lamb or beef stew meat, cut into 1-inch cubes
1 tablespoon cooking oil
3 leeks, cut into 1-inch pieces
1 large onion, chopped
½ cup dry yellow split peas
4 cloves garlic, sliced
2 bay leaves
1 tablespoon snipped fresh oregano or 1 teaspoon dried oregano, crushed
1½ teaspoons ground cumin
¼ teaspoon ground black pepper
3 cups chicken broth
⅓ cup raisins
2 tablespoons lemon juice
3 cups hot cooked bulgur or rice

1. In a large skillet brown meat, half at a time, in hot oil. Drain off fat. Transfer meat to a 3½-, 4-, or 5-quart slow cooker. Stir in leeks, onion, split peas, garlic, bay leaves, dried oregano (if using), cumin, and pepper. Pour chicken broth over all.

2. Cover; cook on low-heat setting for 8 to 10 hours or on high-heat setting for 4 to 5 hours. If using low-heat setting, turn to high-heat setting. Stir raisins into stew. Cover; cook for 15 minutes more. Remove the bay leaves and discard. Stir in lemon juice and, if using, the fresh oregano. Serve with hot bulgur or rice.

Nutrition Facts per serving: 357 calories, 9 g total fat, 58 mg cholesterol, 449 mg sodium, 42 g carbohydrate, 29 g protein.

Brunswick Stew

Early nineteenth-century settlers in Brunswick County, Virginia, created this classic stew that's loaded with vegetables associated with the South: okra, lima beans, and corn.

Prep: 20 minutes **Cook:** 8 hours on low plus 45 minutes on high or 4¾ hours on high **Makes:** 6 servings

1. In a 3½- or 4-quart slow cooker place onion. Top with chicken and ham. In a small bowl combine tomatoes, broth, garlic, Worcestershire sauce, mustard, thyme, pepper, and hot pepper sauce; pour over chicken and ham.

2. Cover; cook on low-heat setting for 8 to 10 hours or on high-heat setting for 4 to 5 hours.

3. If desired, remove chicken; cool slightly. (Keep lid on the slow cooker.) Remove meat from chicken bones; cut meat into bite-size pieces. Return chicken to slow cooker; discard bones.

4. Add okra, lima beans, and corn to slow cooker. If using low-heat setting, turn to high-heat setting. Cover; cook 45 minutes more or until vegetables are tender.

Nutrition Facts per serving: 322 calories, 9 g total fat, 84 mg cholesterol, 990 mg sodium, 24 g carbohydrate, 34 g protein.

3 medium onions, cut into thin wedges

2 pounds meaty chicken pieces, skinned

1½ cups diced cooked ham (8 ounces)

1 14½-ounce can diced tomatoes, undrained

1 14-ounce can chicken broth

4 cloves garlic, minced

1 tablespoon Worcestershire sauce

1 teaspoon dry mustard

1 teaspoon dried thyme, crushed

¼ teaspoon ground black pepper

¼ teaspoon bottled hot pepper sauce

1 10-ounce package frozen sliced okra (2 cups)

1 cup frozen baby lima beans

1 cup frozen whole kernel corn

Chicken and Sausage Gumbo

You can make the roux the night before and keep it in the refrigerator, covered. When cooked, the roux should be a coppery color, similar to a tarnished penny.

Prep: 30 minutes **Cook:** 6 hours on low or 3 hours on high **Makes:** 5 servings

⅓ cup all-purpose flour

⅓ cup cooking oil

3 cups water

12 ounces fully cooked smoked sausage links, quartered lengthwise and sliced

1½ cups chopped cooked chicken or 12 ounces skinless, boneless chicken breasts or thighs, cut into ¾-inch pieces

2 cups sliced okra or one 10-ounce package frozen whole okra, partially thawed and cut into ½-inch slices

1 cup chopped onion

½ cup chopped green sweet pepper

½ cup chopped celery

4 cloves garlic, minced

½ teaspoon salt

½ teaspoon ground black pepper

¼ teaspoon ground red pepper

3 cups hot cooked rice

1. For the roux, in a heavy 2-quart saucepan stir together the flour and oil until smooth. Cook over medium-high heat for 5 minutes, stirring constantly. Reduce heat to medium. Cook and stir constantly about 15 minutes more or until a dark, reddish-brown roux forms. Cool.

2. In a 3-½-, 4-, or 5-quart slow cooker place water. Stir in roux. Add sausage, chicken, okra, onion, sweet pepper, celery, garlic, salt, black pepper, and red pepper.

3. Cover; cook on low-heat setting for 6 to 7 hours or on high-heat setting for 3 to 3½ hours. Skim off fat. Serve over the hot cooked rice.

Nutrition Facts per serving: 637 calories, 39 g total fat, 83 mg cholesterol, 952 mg sodium, 45 g carbohydrate, 28 g protein.

Chicken and Wild Rice Stew

With two kinds of rice, mushrooms, and leeks, this hearty chicken stew makes for earthy and elegant autumn fare. Serve it with a salad of field greens and whole wheat rolls.

Prep: 20 minutes **Cook:** 7 hours on low or 3½ hours on high **Makes:** 6 servings

1. In a 3½-, 4-, 5-, or 6-quart slow cooker place mushrooms, carrots, leeks, and rices. Place chicken on vegetables and rices. Top with thyme, rosemary, and pepper. Pour broth over all.

2. Cover; cook on low-heat setting for 7 to 8 hours or on high-heat setting for 3½ to 4 hours. Stir in mushroom soup.

Nutrition Facts per serving: 264 calories, 6 g total fat, 33 mg cholesterol, 908 mg sodium, 32 g carbohydrate, 22 g protein.

- 3 cups quartered button mushrooms (8 ounces)
- 2 medium carrots, sliced (1 cup)
- 2 medium leeks, sliced (⅔ cup)
- ½ cup uncooked brown rice
- ½ cup uncooked wild rice, rinsed and drained
- 12 ounces skinless, boneless chicken breasts, cut into ¾-inch pieces
- 1 teaspoon dried thyme, crushed
- ½ teaspoon dried rosemary, crushed
- ¼ teaspoon coarsely ground pepper
- 3 14-ounce cans reduced-sodium chicken broth (5¼ cups)
- 1 10¾-ounce can condensed cream of mushroom soup

Shrimp Creole

Creole cooking is a fusion of Spanish, French, and African cuisines that came together in New Orleans. It makes great use of tomatoes, such as those in this sophisticated seafood stew.

Prep: 20 minutes **Cook:** 5 hours on low or 2½ hours on high **Makes:** 6 to 8 servings

1½ cups chopped onion

1 cup chopped green
sweet pepper

2 stalks celery, cut into
½-inch slices (1 cup)

⅓ cup thinly sliced green onion

2 cloves garlic, minced

1 14½-ounce can diced
tomatoes, undrained

1 14-ounce can chicken broth

1 6-ounce can tomato paste

1½ teaspoons paprika

½ teaspoon ground black
pepper

¼ teaspoon salt

1 bay leaf
Several dashes bottled
hot pepper sauce

1½ pounds peeled, deveined,
cooked medium shrimp

3 cups hot cooked rice

1. In a 3½-quart slow cooker place onion, sweet pepper, celery, green onion, garlic, tomatoes, chicken broth, tomato paste, paprika, pepper, salt, bay leaf, and hot pepper sauce. Stir to combine.

2. Cover; cook on low-heat setting for 5 to 6 hours or on high-heat setting for 2½ to 3 hours. Remove bay leaf. Stir in shrimp. Serve over cooked rice.

Nutrition Facts per serving: 344 calories, 3 g total fat, 227 mg cholesterol, 673 mg sodium, 39 g carbohydrate, 37 g protein.

Vegetarian Chili

Between the kidney beans, chunky tomatoes, green pepper, and celery, you won't miss the meat in this highly textured bowl o' red.

Prep: 15 minutes **Cook:** 9 hours on low or 4½ hours on high **Makes:** 6 servings

1. In a 4- or 4½-quart slow cooker place all ingredients. Stir to combine.

2. Cover; cook on low-heat setting for 9 to 10 hours or on high-heat setting for 4½ to 5 hours.

Nutrition Facts per serving: **229 calories, 1 g total fat, 0 mg cholesterol, 1,271 mg sodium, 51 g carbohydrate, 14 g protein.**

3 cups hot-style tomato juice
   or hot-style vegetable juice
2 15-ounce cans red kidney
   beans, rinsed and drained
1 15½-ounce can whole kernel
   corn, drained
1 14½-ounce can chunky
   chili-style tomatoes or one
   14½-ounce can Mexican-
   style stewed tomatoes,
   undrained
1 cup chopped onion
1 cup chopped green
   sweet pepper
1 cup chopped celery
1 clove garlic, minced
1 to 2 teaspoons chili powder
¼ teaspoon salt
¼ teaspoon ground
   black pepper

Hearty Vegetarian Stew

Savory steak sauce (but no steak) gives great flavor to this meatless one-dish meal.

Prep: 15 minutes **Cook:** 9 hours on low or 4½ hours on high **Makes:** 5 servings

1 pound potatoes, cut into
    1-inch cubes
1 large onion, chopped
    (1 cup)
2 medium carrots, sliced
    (1 cup)
1 15-ounce can red kidney
    beans, rinsed and drained
1 15-ounce can tomato sauce
1 14½-ounce can diced
    tomatoes with basil, garlic,
    and oregano; undrained
1 10-ounce package frozen
    whole kernel corn
2 teaspoons steak sauce
⅔ cup shredded cheddar
    cheese

1. In a 3½- or 4-quart slow cooker combine potatoes, onion, carrots, beans, tomato sauce, tomatoes, corn, and steak sauce.

2. Cover; cook on low-heat setting for 9 to 11 hours or on high-heat setting for 4½ to 5½ hours. To serve, sprinkle cheese over stew.

Nutrition Facts per serving: 325 calories, 6 g total fat, 16 mg cholesterol, 1,219 mg sodium, 60 g carbohydrate, 16 g protein.

Vegetable-Patch Chili

Some like it hot—some don't. If you're in the latter group, use regular stewed tomatoes and a mild salsa in this meatless chili. Serve it with warm cornmeal biscuits.

Prep: 15 minutes **Cook:** 8 hours on low or 4 hours on high **Makes:** 4 servings

1. In a 3½- or 4-quart slow cooker combine zucchini, sweet pepper, onion, celery, garlic, chili powder, oregano, and cumin. Stir in tomatoes, corn, beans, and salsa.

2. Cover; cook on low-heat setting for 8 to 10 hours or on high-heat setting for 4 to 5 hours. To serve, ladle the chili into bowls and top with a small amount of sour cream.

Nutrition Facts per serving: **277 calories, 7 g total fat, 6 mg cholesterol, 1,599 mg sodium, 54 g carbohydrate, 13 g protein.**

1 medium zucchini, cut into
 ½-inch pieces (1½ cups)
1 medium green sweet pepper,
 coarsely chopped (1 cup)
½ cup coarsely chopped onion
½ cup coarsely chopped celery
2 cloves garlic, minced
2 to 3 teaspoons chili powder
1 teaspoon dried oregano,
 crushed
½ teaspoon ground cumin
2 14½-ounce cans Mexican-
 style stewed tomatoes,
 undrained
1 17-ounce can whole
 kernel corn, undrained
1 15-ounce can black beans,
 rinsed and drained
1 8-ounce jar salsa
 Dairy sour cream

meats

Enjoy family favorites such as melt-in-your-mouth pot roast,
homestyle meat loaf, or falling-off-the-bone barbecued ribs—or put
on a company-special meal of lamb or veal—any day of the week.

Tangy Barbecue Beef, page 108

Pot Roast with Basil Mashed Potatoes

Melt-in-your-mouth pot roast and basil-infused mashed potatoes are just the thing for a comfort-food-to-the-max dinner after a long, hard day.

Prep: 25 minutes **Cook:** 8 hours on low or 4 hours on high **Stand:** 10 minutes **Makes:** 6 servings

2 carrots, cut into ½-inch pieces (1 cup)

1 medium turnip, peeled and cubed (1 cup)

1 small onion, chopped

½ cup snipped dried tomatoes (not oil-packed)

1 clove garlic, minced

1 teaspoon instant beef bouillon granules

½ teaspoon dried basil, crushed

½ teaspoon dried oregano, crushed

⅛ teaspoon ground black pepper

1 1½-to 2-pound boneless beef chuck pot roast

1 cup water

1 10-ounce package frozen lima beans or whole kernel corn

1 cup frozen peas

1 20-ounce package refrigerated mashed potatoes

1 tablespoon finely snipped fresh basil

1. In a 3½- or 4-quart slow cooker combine the carrots, turnip, onion, tomatoes, garlic, bouillon granules, dried basil, oregano, and pepper. Trim fat from meat. If necessary, cut roast to fit into cooker. Place meat on vegetables. Pour water over all.

2. Cover; cook on low-heat setting for 8 to 10 hours or on high-heat setting for 4 to 5 hours. Stir in lima beans and peas. Let stand, covered, for 10 minutes.

3. Meanwhile, prepare mashed potatoes according to package directions, except stir the 1 tablespoon fresh basil into potatoes just before serving. Remove meat and vegetables from cooker with a slotted spoon. If desired, reserve cooking juices. Serve meat and vegetables over hot mashed potatoes. If desired, serve cooking juices over meat.

Nutrition Facts per serving: 436 calories, 12 g total fat, 87 mg cholesterol, 497 mg sodium, 46 g carbohydrate, 35 g protein.

Beef Stroganoff

Considered classic company fare in the 1960s, time hasn't changed the elegance of this stew that features tender chunks of beef in a rich herbed sauce on a bed of egg noodles.

Prep: 25 minutes **Cook:** 8 hours on low plus 30 minutes on high or 4½ hours on high **Makes:** 6 servings

1. In a large skillet brown beef, half at a time, in hot oil. Drain off fat.

2. In a 3½-quart slow cooker combine beef, mushrooms, onion, garlic, oregano, salt, thyme, pepper, and bay leaf. Pour beef broth and sherry over all.

3. Cover; cook on low-heat setting for 8 to 10 hours or on high-heat setting for 4 to 5 hours. Discard bay leaf.

4. If using low-heat setting, turn to high-heat setting. Mix together sour cream, flour, and water. Stir about 1 cup of the hot liquid into sour cream mixture. Return all to cooker; stir to combine. Cover; cook on high-heat setting for 30 minutes or until thickened and bubbly.

5. Serve over hot cooked noodles or rice. If desired, sprinkle with snipped fresh parsley.

Nutrition Facts per serving: 497 calories, 20 g total fat, 135 mg cholesterol, 368 mg sodium, 38 g carbohydrate, 36 g protein.

1½ pounds beef stew meat, cut into 1-inch cubes
1 tablespoon cooking oil
2 cups sliced fresh mushrooms
½ cup sliced green onions
2 cloves garlic, minced
½ teaspoon dried oregano, crushed
¼ teaspoon salt
¼ teaspoon dried thyme, crushed
¼ teaspoon ground black pepper
1 bay leaf
1½ cups beef broth
⅓ cup dry sherry
1 8-ounce carton dairy sour cream
½ cup all-purpose flour
¼ cup water
4 cups hot cooked noodles or rice
Snipped fresh parsley (optional)

Cajun Pot Roast

If you can't find Cajun seasoning, mix together 1 to 1½ teaspoons seasoned salt, ½ to ¾ teaspoon ground red pepper, and ½ to ¾ teaspoon ground black pepper.

Prep: 25 minutes **Cook:** 10 hours on low or 5 hours on high **Makes:** 6 servings

---

1 2- to 2½-pound boneless
    beef chuck pot roast
2 to 3 teaspoons Cajun
    seasoning
1 tablespoon cooking oil
1 14½-ounce can Cajun-style
    or Mexican-style stewed
    tomatoes, undrained
1 cup chopped onion
1 cup chopped celery
¼ cup quick-cooking tapioca
1 teaspoon bottled minced
    garlic or 2 cloves garlic,
    minced
    Hot cooked rice

1. Trim fat from roast. Cut roast to fit in slow cooker, if necessary. Rub Cajun seasoning all over meat. In a large skillet brown meat on all sides in hot oil.

2. In a 3½- to 4-quart slow cooker combine tomatoes, onion, celery, tapioca, and garlic. Place meat on top of vegetable mixture.

3. Cover; cook on low-heat setting for 10 to 12 hours or on high-heat setting for 5 to 6 hours.

4. Slice meat; serve with sauce over rice.

Make-Ahead Tip: This mildly spiced meat and sauce also make a delicious hot sandwich. Using 2 forks, shred any leftover meat. Combine the shredded beef and remaining sauce in a storage container; cover and freeze for up to 3 months. Thaw mixture overnight in the refrigerator. Pour into a saucepan and heat through. Serve on hard rolls with sliced tomato and sliced green onion.

Nutrition Facts per serving: **273 calories, 7 g total fat, 55 mg cholesterol, 366 mg sodium, 31 g carbohydrate, 21 g protein.**

Beef Brisket in Beer

Slow cooking is the key to tenderizing tougher cuts of meat, such as brisket. After simmering in a slow cooker all day, you won't even need a butter knife to dig into this beef-and-onion dish.

Prep: 15 minutes **Cook:** 10 hours on low or 5 hours on high **Makes:** 10 servings

1. Trim fat from brisket. If necessary, cut brisket to fit into cooker. In a 3½-, 4-, 5-, or 6-quart slow cooker place onions, bay leaf, and brisket. Combine beer, chili sauce, sugar, thyme, salt, pepper, and garlic; pour over brisket. Cover; cook on low-heat setting for 10 to 12 hours or high-heat setting 5 to 6 hours.

2. Transfer brisket and onions to a platter; keep warm. Discard bay leaf. For gravy, skim fat from cooking juices. Measure 2½ cups juices and place in a saucepan. Combine cornstarch and water; add to saucepan. Cook and stir until thick and bubbly; cook and stir 2 minutes more. Pass gravy with meat.

Nutrition Facts per serving: 227 calories, 7 g total fat, 78 mg cholesterol, 242 mg sodium, 8 g carbohydrate, 30 g protein.

1 3 to 4-pound fresh
   beef brisket
2 onions, thinly sliced and
   separated into rings
1 bay leaf
1 cup beer
¼ cup chili sauce
2 tablespoons packed brown
   sugar
½ teaspoon dried thyme,
   crushed
¼ teaspoon salt
¼ teaspoon ground black
   pepper
1 clove garlic, minced
2 tablespoons cornstarch
2 tablespoons water

Beef Burgundy

Using the reduced-fat versions of the cream soups cuts down on fat grams, but not on flavor.

Prep: 25 minutes **Cook:** 8 hours on low or 4 hours on high **Makes:** 6 servings

1½ pounds beef stew meat, cut
    into 1-inch cubes
2 tablespoons cooking oil
1 10¾-ounce can condensed
    cream of celery soup or
    reduced-fat and reduced-
    sodium condensed cream
    of celery soup
1 10¾-ounce can condensed
    cream of mushroom soup
    or reduced-fat and
    reduced-sodium condensed
    cream of mushroom soup
¾ cup Burgundy wine
1 envelope onion soup mix
    (½ of a 2.2-ounce package)
8 ounces fresh mushrooms,
    sliced (3 cups)
    Hot cooked noodles or rice

1. In a large skillet brown the meat, half at a time, in hot oil. Drain off fat.

2. In a 3½-, 4-, or 5-quart slow cooker combine celery soup, mushroom soup, Burgundy, onion soup mix, and mushrooms. Stir in browned meat. Cover; cook on low-heat setting for 8 to 10 hours or on high-heat setting for 4 to 5 hours. Serve over noodles or rice.

Nutrition Facts per serving: 435 calories, 18 g total fat, 60 mg cholesterol, 985 mg sodium, 33 g carbohydrate, 30 g protein.

French Dips with Portobellos

Meaty portobello mushrooms add a new dimension to classic French dip sandwiches. Serve the seasoned broth in bowls just large enough to dunk a corner of the sandwich.

Prep: 25 minutes **Cook:** 8 hours on low or 4 hours on high **Stand:** 10 minutes **Makes:** 8 sandwiches

1. Trim fat from roast. If necessary, cut roast to fit into a 3½-, 4-, 5-, or 6-quart slow cooker. In a large skillet brown meat on all sides in hot oil. Drain off fat. Transfer meat to cooker.

2. Clean mushrooms; remove and discard stems. Cut mushrooms into ¼-inch slices. Add to cooker. Pour broth over meat and mushrooms.

3. Cover; cook on low-heat setting for 8 to 9 hours or on high-heat setting for 4 to 4½ hours. Remove meat from cooker; cover and let stand for 10 minutes.

4. Meanwhile, using a slotted spoon, remove mushrooms and set aside. Thinly slice meat. Arrange meat, mushrooms and onion slices on toasted buns. Pour cooking juices into a measuring cup; skim off fat. Drizzle a little of the juices onto each sandwich and pour the remaining juices into individual bowls; serve with sandwiches for dipping.

Nutrition Facts per serving: 780 calories, 33 g total fat, 106 mg cholesterol, 955 mg sodium, 73 g carbohydrate, 47 g protein.

1 3- to 3½-pound beef bottom round or rump roast
1 tablespoon cooking oil
4 portobello mushrooms (3 to 4 inches in diameter)
1 14½-ounce can beef broth seasoned with onion
8 hoagie buns, split and toasted
1 large red onion, cut into ½ inch slices

Tangy Barbecue Beef

Sweet slices of mango add a fresh touch to these barbecued beef sandwiches. To save time, look for prepeeled and sliced mango in the refrigerator case of the grocery produce section.

Prep: 25 minutes **Cook:** 10 hours on low **Stand:** 15 minutes **Makes:** 8 servings

1 3-pound fresh beef brisket, trimmed

2 tablespoons chili powder

1 teaspoon celery seeds

½ teaspoon salt

½ teaspoon freshly ground black pepper

2 onions, thinly sliced

1 cup bottled smoke-flavored barbecue sauce

½ cup beer or ginger ale

8 large sandwich buns or Portuguese rolls, split and toasted

Bottled hot pepper sauce (optional)

Mango slices

1. Trim fat from brisket. In a small bowl combine the chili powder, celery seeds, salt, and pepper. Rub the spice mixture onto all sides of the brisket. Scatter half of the sliced onions in the bottom of a 3½-, 4-, 5-, or 6-quart slow cooker. Place the brisket on the onions, cutting the meat to fit, if necessary. Scatter the remaining onions on top of the brisket. In a small bowl stir together the barbecue sauce and beer. Pour over the brisket and onions.

2. Cover; cook on low-heat setting for 10 to 12 hours or until meat is fork-tender. Transfer meat to a cutting board and let stand for 15 minutes. Halve meat crosswise. Using 2 forks, pull meat apart into shreds. Return meat to sauce mixture in slow cooker. Heat through using the high-heat setting.

3. To serve, use a slotted spoon to transfer beef and onion mixture into the buns. If desired, season to taste with hot pepper sauce. Top with mango slices. (Freeze any remaining beef mixture in a freezer container for up to 3 months.)

Nutrition Facts per serving: 442 calories, 11 g total fat, 98 mg cholesterol, 971 mg sodium, 41 g carbohydrate, 41 g protein.

Sunday Dinner Pot Roast

If you're looking for a pot roast like Mom used to make, this is it: potatoes, mushrooms, carrots, and herbs in a creamy mushroom sauce.

Prep: 15 minutes **Cook:** 10 hours on low **Makes:** 5 servings

1. Trim fat from meat. Spray an unheated large skillet with cooking spray. Add meat and brown on all sides.

2. Place potatoes, mushrooms, carrots, and tarragon in a 3½- or 4-quart slow cooker. Place browned meat on top of vegetables. Sprinkle with salt. Pour soup over meat. Cover; cook on low-heat setting for 10 to 12 hours.

3. To serve, transfer meat and vegetables to a serving platter. Serve the sauce over meat and vegetables.

Nutrition Facts per serving: 437 calories, 17 g total fat, 102 mg cholesterol, 780 mg sodium, 37 g carbohydrate, 35 g protein.

1 1½-pound boneless beef chuck eye roast, eye of round roast, or round rump roast
Nonstick cooking spray

4 medium potatoes, unpeeled and quartered

1 4-ounce can mushroom stems and pieces, drained

2 cups packaged, peeled baby carrots

½ teaspoon dried tarragon or basil, crushed

¼ teaspoon salt

1 10¾-ounce can condensed mushroom soup

Short Ribs with Leeks

The best way to clean leeks—which can be gritty—is to cut off the tops and bottoms then cut them lengthwise down the middle. Run each half under cold water, fanning the layers.

Prep: 30 minutes **Cook:** 7 hours on low or 3½ hours on high **Makes:** 6 servings

8 ounces fresh mushrooms,
  halved
4 medium carrots, cut into
  1-inch pieces (2 cups)
4 medium leeks, cut into
  1-inch slices
2 pounds boneless beef
  short ribs
2 teaspoons finely shredded
  lemon peel
½ teaspoon ground black
  pepper
½ teaspoon dried rosemary,
  crushed
½ teaspoon dried thyme,
  crushed
¼ teaspoon salt
¾ cup beef broth
⅓ cup dairy sour cream
1 tablespoon all-purpose flour

1. Place mushrooms, carrots, and leeks in a 3½- or 4-quart slow cooker. Place beef over vegetables. Sprinkle with lemon peel, pepper, rosemary, thyme, and salt. Add broth. Cover; cook on low-heat setting for 7 to 8 hours or on high-heat setting for 3½ to 4 hours.

2. Use a slotted spoon to transfer meat and vegetables to serving dish. Cover and keep warm.

3. Skim fat from remaining cooking liquid. Measure 1 cup cooking liquid. Place in a small saucepan. In a small bowl stir together sour cream and flour. Stir into cooking liquid using a whisk. Cook and stir over medium heat until slightly thickened and bubbly; cook and stir for 1 minute more. Ladle sauce over meat and vegetables.

Nutrition Facts per serving: 173 calories, 8 g total fat, 33 mg cholesterol, 252 mg sodium, 10 g carbohydrate, 15 g protein.

Beef and Peppers Sandwiches

Just serve cut-up, fresh vegetables and a light dip as a sidecar to these Italian-style beef sandwiches, and dinner is on the table.

Prep: 10 minutes **Cook:** 10 hours on low plus 30 minutes on high or 5½ hours on high **Broil:** 1 minute **Makes:** 8 servings

1. In a 3½- or 4-quart slow cooker combine meat, onion, Worcestershire sauce, bouillon granules, oregano, basil, thyme, and garlic.

2. Cover; cook on low-heat setting for 10 hours or on high-heat setting for 5 to 6 hours. Stir to break up meat cubes. Stir in pepperoncini. Cook, uncovered, on high-heat setting for 30 minutes more, stirring often to break up meat.

3. Preheat broiler. Using a slotted spoon, place meat mixture on the bottom halves of buns. Top each sandwich with cheese. Broil sandwiches 4 inches from heat about 1 minute or until cheese melts. Add top halves of buns.

Nutrition Facts per serving: 493 calories, 18 g total fat, 122 mg cholesterol, 1,009 mg sodium, 35 g carbohydrate, 46 g protein.

1 2½- to 3-pound boneless beef chuck pot roast, cut into 1-inch cubes
1 large onion, chopped
¼ cup Worcestershire sauce
1 tablespoon instant beef bouillon granules
1 teaspoon dried oregano, crushed
½ teaspoon dried basil, crushed
½ teaspoon dried thyme, crushed
2 cloves garlic, minced
½ cup chopped pepperoncini (Italian pickled peppers) or other pickled peppers
8 hoagie buns or kaiser rolls, split and toasted
6 ounces sliced Swiss cheese

Beef and Vegetables in Red Wine Sauce

Use a hearty red wine, such as a Cabernet Sauvignon or Merlot, to make this delicious dish—

and enjoy it with a glass of the same.

Prep: 25 minutes **Cook:** 8 hours on low or 4 hours on high **Makes:** 6 to 8 servings

1½ pounds boneless beef
     bottom round steak,
     cut into 1-inch cubes
1 tablespoon cooking oil
2 medium carrots, cut into
     ½-inch pieces (1 cup)
2 stalks celery, cut into
     ½-inch pieces (1 cup)
1 cup quartered fresh
     mushrooms
½ cup sliced green onions
3 tablespoons quick-cooking
     tapioca
1 14½-ounce can Italian-style
     stewed tomatoes,
     undrained
1 cup beef broth
½ cup dry red wine, white
     wine, or beef broth
1 teaspoon dried Italian
     seasoning, crushed
½ teaspoon salt
¼ teaspoon ground black
     pepper
1 bay leaf
3 cups hot cooked noodles

1. In a large skillet brown beef, half at a time, in hot oil. Drain off fat.

2. Transfer beef to a 3½- or 4-quart slow cooker. Add carrots, celery, mushrooms, and green onion. Sprinkle with tapioca.

3. Combine undrained tomatoes, beef broth, wine, Italian seasoning, salt, pepper, and bay leaf. Pour over vegetables and meat.

4. Cover; cook on low-heat setting for 8 to 10 hours or on high-heat setting for 4 to 5 hours. Discard bay leaf. Serve over hot cooked noodles.

Nutrition Facts per serving: 365 calories, 9 g total fat, 98 mg cholesterol, 662 mg sodium, 34 g carbohydrate, 33 g protein.

Beef Brisket with Smoky Barbecue Sauce

Serve this smoky, saucy beef on buns or rolls. Round out the meal with baked beans and coleslaw.

Prep: 15 minutes **Cook:** 8 hours on low or 4 hours on high **Makes:** 6 to 8 servings

1. Trim fat from brisket. If necessary, cut brisket to fit into slow cooker.

2. Combine chili powder, garlic powder, celery seeds, and pepper; rub evenly over meat. Place meat in a 3½-, 4-, or 5-quart slow cooker.

3. For sauce, combine ketchup, chili sauce, brown sugar, vinegar, Worcestershire sauce, Liquid Smoke, and dry mustard. Pour sauce over brisket.

4. Cover; cook on low-heat setting for 8 to 10 hours or on high-heat setting for 4 to 5 hours. Remove meat from cooker. Cut the brisket into thin slices across the grain. Skim fat off juices in cooker; serve juices with meat.

Nutrition Facts per serving: 358 calories, 15 g total fat, 104 mg cholesterol, 676 mg sodium, 22 g carbohydrate, 34 g protein.

1 2- to 3-pound fresh
  beef brisket
1 teaspoon chili powder
½ teaspoon garlic powder
¼ teaspoon celery seeds
⅛ teaspoon ground black
  pepper
½ cup ketchup
½ cup chili sauce
¼ cup packed brown sugar
2 tablespoons vinegar
2 tablespoons Worcestershire
  sauce
1½ teaspoons Liquid Smoke
½ teaspoon dry mustard

Herbed Mushroom Round Steak

Bottom round steak—which is more economical than tip round steak—is a great choice for a slow cooker because the moist heat tenderizes the meat.

Prep: 20 minutes **Cook:** 8 hours on low or 4 hours on high **Makes:** 6 servings

2 pounds beef round steak,
  cut ¾ inch thick
1 tablespoon cooking oil
1 medium onion, sliced
2 cups sliced fresh
  mushrooms or two 4-ounce
  jars canned mushrooms;
  drained
1 10¾-ounce can condensed
  cream of mushroom soup
¼ cup dry white wine
  (optional)
½ teaspoon dried oregano,
  crushed
¼ teaspoon dried thyme,
  crushed
¼ teaspoon ground black
  pepper
3 cups hot cooked noodles

1. Trim fat from meat. Cut meat into serving-size portions. In a large skillet brown beef on both sides in hot oil.

2. In a 3½- or 4-quart slow cooker place onion and mushrooms. Place beef on top of vegetables.

3. In a small bowl combine soup, wine (if desired), oregano, thyme, and pepper; pour over meat.

4. Cover; cook on low-heat setting for 8 to 10 hours or on high-heat setting for 4 to 5 hours. Serve over hot cooked noodles.

Nutrition Facts per serving: 414 calories, 15 g total fat, 123 mg cholesterol, 488 mg sodium, 27 g carbohydrate, 42 g protein.

Rump Roast and Vegetables

No stirring needed: A delicious gravy forms as the roast and vegetables slowly simmer.

Serve them with mashed potatoes or soft rolls to sop up every last bite of the delicious stuff.

Prep: 20 minutes **Cook:** 10 hours on low or 5 hours on high **Makes:** 6 servings

1. If necessary, cut roast to fit into the slow cooker. In a large skillet brown roast on all sides in hot oil. Meanwhile, in a 3½-, 4-, 5-, or 6-quart slow cooker place potatoes, carrots, and onion. Add beans and bay leaf. Sprinkle tapioca over vegetables. Place roast on top of vegetables.

2. In a medium bowl combine condensed soup, water, and pepper; pour over roast. Cover; cook on low-heat setting for 10 to 12 hours or on high-heat setting for 5 to 6 hours.

3. To serve, discard bay leaf and remove any strings from roast. Arrange roast and vegetables on a warm serving platter. Skim fat from gravy. Spoon some of the gravy over roast; pass remaining gravy with roast and vegetables.

Nutrition Facts per serving: 432 calories, 12 g total fat, 82 mg cholesterol, 460 mg sodium, 38 g carbohydrate, 43 g protein.

- 1 2- to 2½-pound boneless beef round rump, round tip, or chuck pot roast
- 2 tablespoons cooking oil
- 1½ pounds small potatoes (about 10) or medium potatoes (about 4), halved
- 2 medium carrots, cut into ½-inch pieces (1 cup)
- 1 small onion, sliced
- 1 10-ounce package frozen lima beans
- 1 bay leaf
- 2 tablespoons quick-cooking tapioca
- 1 10¾-ounce can condensed vegetable beef soup
- ¼ cup water
- ¼ teaspoon ground black pepper

Hungarian Goulash

Hungarian paprika is considered superior to paprikas produced in other parts of the world. Either sweet or hot paprika can be used in this classic dish.

Prep: 25 minutes **Cook:** 9½ hours on low plus 30 minutes on high or 4 hours on high **Makes:** 6 servings

1½ pounds beef stew meat,
   cut into 1-inch cubes
1 tablespoon cooking oil
2 medium carrots, bias-sliced
   into ½-inch pieces (1 cup)
2 medium onions, thinly sliced
3 cloves garlic, minced
1¼ cups beef broth
1 6-ounce can tomato paste
1 tablespoon Hungarian
   paprika
1 teaspoon finely shredded
   lemon peel
½ teaspoon salt
½ teaspoon caraway seeds
¼ teaspoon ground
   black pepper
1 bay leaf
1 green sweet pepper,
   cut into strips
1 red or green sweet pepper,
   cut into strips
3 cups hot cooked noodles
   Dairy sour cream or yogurt

1. In a large skillet brown beef, half at a time, in hot oil. Drain fat.

2. Transfer meat to a 3½- or 4-quart slow cooker. Add carrots, onions, and garlic. In a small bowl combine beef broth, tomato paste, paprika, lemon peel, salt, caraway seeds, black pepper, and bay leaf. Stir into vegetable-meat mixture.

3. Cover; cook on low-heat setting for 9½ to 11½ hours or on high-heat setting for 3½ to 4½ hours.

4. If using low-heat setting, turn to high-heat setting. Stir in sweet pepper strips. Cover; cook 30 minutes longer on high-heat setting. Discard bay leaf. Serve with hot cooked noodles and a small amount of sour cream or yogurt.

Nutrition Facts per serving: **391 calories, 13 g total fat, 115 mg cholesterol, 442 mg sodium, 34 g carbohydrate, 34 g protein.**

Country Swiss Steak

"Swissing" is a term that refers to the process of smoothing cloth between rollers. In this recipe, the phrase likely refers to the pounding and flattening of the meat in traditional Swiss steak.

Prep: 15 minutes **Cook:** 10 hours on low or 5 hours on high **Makes:** 4 servings

1. Trim fat from meat. Cut meat into 4 serving-size pieces. In a skillet, brown meat and sausage in hot oil. In a 3½- or 4-quart slow cooker place onion. Sprinkle with thyme, tapioca, salt, and pepper. Pour tomatoes over vegetables. Add meat.

2. Cover; cook on low-heat setting for 10 to 12 hours or on high-heat setting for 4 to 5 hours. Serve with hot cooked noodles or rice. If desired, sprinkle with thyme sprigs.

Nutrition Facts per serving: **412 calories, 15 g total fat, 110 mg cholesterol, 755 mg sodium, 32 g carbohydrate, 35 g protein.**

1 pound boneless beef round steak, cut 1 inch thick
4 ounces spicy fresh bratwurst or other sausage, cut into ¾-inch slices
1 tablespoon cooking oil
1 small onion, sliced and separated into rings
1 teaspoon dried thyme, crushed
2 tablespoons quick-cooking tapioca
½ teaspoon salt
¼ teaspoon ground black pepper
1 14½-ounce can chunky tomatoes with olive oil, garlic, and spices; undrained
2 cups hot cooked noodles or rice
Fresh thyme sprigs (optional)

Philadelphia Cheesesteak Wraps

A favorite street food is just as good eaten at the table for a quick dinner.

Serve these hearty wraps with a fresh fruit salad.

Prep: 20 minutes **Cook:** 10 hours on low or 5 hours on high **Makes:** 6 servings

1 tablespoon cooking oil
1 pound beef flank steak
1 cup red sweet pepper strips
1 cup thin onion wedges
1½ teaspoons dried Italian seasoning, crushed
1 14-ounce can beef broth
½ cup mayonnaise
4 teaspoons prepared horseradish
6 10-inch flour tortillas
3 slices provolone cheese slices, halved

1. In a large skillet, heat oil over medium-high heat. Add flank steak and brown well on both sides. Place pepper strips, onion wedges, and Italian seasoning in a 4- or 5-quart slow cooker. Top with flank steak. Pour beef broth over all.

2. Cover; cook on low-heat setting for 10 to 12 hours or on high-heat setting for 5 to 6 hours.

3. Remove flank steak from slow cooker and shred the meat. Combine mayonnaise and horseradish; spread on each flour tortilla. Place sliced meat along the center of each tortilla. Remove pepper and onion mixture from slow cooker with a slotted spoon and place on top of beef. Place a half slice of provolone on top. Roll tightly.

Nutrition Facts per serving: 484 calories, 30 g total fat, 48 mg cholesterol, 627 mg sodium, 27 g carbohydrate, 25 g protein.

Port Wine Pot Roast

The rich, seasoned gravy is terrific over hot cooked noodles or mashed potatoes. Just add a crisp lettuce salad or steamed green beans to complete the meal.

Prep: 15 minutes   **Cook:** 8 hours on low or 4 hours on high   **Makes:** 8 to 10 servings

---

1. Trim fat from pot roast. If necessary, cut roast to fit into a 3½- or 4-quart slow cooker. Place meat in cooker.

2. In a small bowl combine onion, port, tomato sauce, tapioca, Worcestershire, thyme, oregano, and garlic. Pour over pot roast.

3. Cover; cook on low-heat setting for 8 to 10 hours or on high-heat setting for 4 to 5 hours. Transfer roast to a serving platter. Skim fat from gravy. Pass gravy with meat. Serve with hot cooked noodles.

Nutrition Facts per serving: 426 calories, 20 g total fat, 104 mg cholesterol, 229 mg sodium, 29 g carbohydrate, 27 g protein.

1 2½- to 3-pound beef chuck
  pot roast
½ cup chopped onion
½ cup port wine or apple juice
1 8-ounce can tomato sauce
3 tablespoons quick-cooking
  tapioca
1 tablespoon Worcestershire
  sauce
1 teaspoon dried thyme,
  crushed
1 teaspoon dried oregano,
  crushed
2 cloves garlic, minced
4 cups hot cooked noodles

Ginger Beef with Broccoli

Bursting with the flavors and fixings of a traditional stir-fry, this easy beef and veggie combo is cloaked in a sauce that begins with an envelope of gravy mix.

Prep: 20 minutes **Cook:** 8 hours on low plus 15 minutes on high or 4¼ hours on high **Makes:** 6 servings

6 medium carrots, cut into 1-inch pieces (3 cups)

2 medium onions, cut into wedges

1½ pounds beef round steak, cut into ½-inch bias-sliced strips

1 tablespoon minced fresh ginger

2 cloves garlic, minced

½ cup water

2 tablespoons reduced-sodium soy sauce

1 ¾-ounce envelope beef gravy mix

4 cups broccoli florets

3 cups hot cooked rice

1. In a 3½- or 4-quart slow cooker place carrots, onions, beef strips, ginger, and garlic. Stir together water, soy sauce, and beef gravy mix. Pour over meat and vegetables in cooker.

2. Cover; cook on low-heat setting for 8 to 10 hours or on high-heat setting for 4 to 5 hours.

3. If using low-heat setting, turn to high-heat setting. Stir in broccoli. Cover and cook 15 minutes more on high-heat setting or until broccoli is crisp-tender. Serve over hot cooked rice.

Nutrition Facts per serving: 327 calories, 6 g total fat, 54 mg cholesterol, 476 mg sodium, 37 g carbohydrate, 31 g protein.

Beef-and-Bean Medley

Served over corn chips and topped with shredded cheddar, this zesty three-bean and beef combo is sure to please even the pickiest eaters.

Prep: 25 minutes **Cook:** 4 hours on low or 2 hours on high **Makes:** 8 to 10 servings

1. In a large skillet cook ground beef and onion until beef is brown. Drain off fat. Transfer beef mixture to a 3½- or 4-quart slow cooker. Add bacon, baked beans, butter beans, and kidney beans. In a small bowl combine ketchup, water, brown sugar, vinegar, and pepper. Add ketchup mixture to slow cooker. Stir to combine. Cover; cook on low-heat setting for 4 to 6 hours or on high-heat setting for 2 to 3 hours.

2. Serve over or with corn chips. Sprinkle with shredded cheese and green onion.

Nutrition Facts per serving: 664 calories, 32 g total fat, 74 mg cholesterol, 1,505 mg sodium, 65 g carbohydrate, 31 g protein.

- 1 pound ground beef
- 1 cup chopped onion
- 6 slices bacon, crisp-cooked, drained, and crumbled
- 2 16-ounce cans baked beans
- 1 15-ounce can butter beans, rinsed and drained
- 1 15-ounce can red kidney beans, rinsed and drained
- 1 cup ketchup
- ½ cup water
- ¼ cup packed brown sugar
- 3 tablespoons vinegar
- ⅛ teaspoon ground black pepper
- 1 8- to 10-ounce bag corn chips or tortilla chips
- 2 cups shredded cheddar cheese (8 ounces)
- ½ cup sliced green onion

Nacho-Style Casserole

Refrigerated sliced potatoes and condensed cheese soup make quick work of preparing this fun layered casserole. Top each serving with sour cream, salsa, and green onions.

Prep: 20 minutes **Cook:** 4 hours on low or 2½ hours on high **Makes:** 4 servings

12 ounces lean ground beef

½ cup chopped onion

1 11-ounce can condensed
   fiesta nacho cheese soup

1 4-ounce can diced green
   chile peppers, undrained

½ cup milk

1 20-ounce package
   refrigerated sliced potatoes

Dairy sour cream (optional)

Salsa (optional)

Sliced green onions
   (optional)

1. In a large skillet cook ground beef and onion until meat is brown. Drain fat. In a medium bowl, stir together the soup, chile peppers, and milk.

2. In a 3½-, 4-, or 5-quart slow cooker layer half of the potatoes, half of the ground beef mixture, and half of the soup mixture. Repeat layers.

3. Cover; cook on low-heat setting for 4 hours or on high-heat setting for 2½ hours or until potatoes are tender. Gently stir before serving. If desired, serve with sour cream, salsa, and sliced green onion.

Nutrition Facts per serving: 368 calories, 16 g total fat, 66 mg cholesterol, 866 mg sodium, 31 g carbohydrate, 23 g protein.

Italian Steak Rolls

Pretty to look at and delicious to eat, these veggie-stuffed steak spirals are perfect for casual entertaining. Just add a salad and some good bread.

Prep: 30 minutes **Cook:** 7 hours on low or 3½ hours on high **Makes:** 6 servings

1. Trim fat from meat. Cut meat into 6 portions. Place the meat between 2 pieces of plastic wrap and, with a meat mallet, pound steak to a ⅛- to ¼-inch thickness.

2. In a small bowl combine carrot, zucchini, sweet pepper, green onion, Parmesan cheese, parsley, garlic, and black pepper. Spoon ⅙ of the vegetable filling on each piece of meat. Roll up meat around the filling and tie each roll with string or secure with wooden toothpicks.

3. Brown meat rolls on all sides in hot oil. Transfer meat rolls to a 3½- or 4-quart slow cooker. Pour spaghetti sauce over the meat rolls.

4. Cover; cook on low-heat setting for 7 to 8 hours or on high-heat setting for 3½ to 4 hours. Discard string or toothpicks. Serve meat rolls with hot cooked pasta.

Nutrition Facts per serving: 358 calories, 10 g total fat, 74 mg cholesterol, 341 mg sodium, 32 g carbohydrate, 33 g protein.

1½ to 2 pounds boneless
    beef round steak
½ cup grated carrot
⅓ cup chopped zucchini
⅓ cup chopped red
    or green sweet pepper
¼ cup sliced green onion
2 tablespoons grated Parmesan
    cheese
1 tablespoon snipped
    fresh parsley
1 clove garlic, minced
¼ teaspoon ground black
    pepper
1 tablespoon cooking oil
1 14-ounce jar meatless
    spaghetti sauce
6 ounces pasta, cooked
    and drained

Deviled Steak Strips

If you don't like the tiny granules of tapioca in the finished dish, grind the tapioca with a mortar and pestle, in a coffee grinder, or blender container for a smoother sauce.

Prep: 15 minutes **Cook:** 7 hours on low or 3½ hours on high **Makes:** 6 to 8 servings

2 pounds boneless beef
    round steak
1 cup chopped onion
3 cloves garlic, minced
1 cup water
1 16-ounce can tomato sauce
3 tablespoons horseradish
    mustard
¼ teaspoon ground black
    pepper
2 teaspoons instant beef
    bouillon granules
3 tablespoons quick-cooking
    tapioca
    Hot cooked noodles, rice,
    or mashed potatoes

1. Cut steak across the grain into bite-size strips. In a 3½- or 4-quart slow cooker place steak strips, onion, garlic, water, tomato sauce, mustard, pepper, bouillon granules, and tapioca. Stir to combine.

2. Cover; cook on low-heat setting for 7 to 9 hours or on high-heat setting for 3½ to 4½ hours. Serve over hot cooked noodles, rice, or mashed potatoes.

Nutrition Facts per serving: 324 calories, 4 g total fat, 86 mg cholesterol, 754 mg sodium, 32 g carbohydrate, 38 g protein.

Beefy Mexican Macaroni with Cheese

Kids will love this fun take on macaroni and cheese.

Prep: 20 minutes **Cook:** 8¼ hours on low or 4¼ hours on high **Makes:** 4 to 6 servings

1. In a large skillet cook ground beef and onion until meat is brown and onion is tender. Drain off fat.

2. Meanwhile, in a 3½- or 4-quart slow cooker combine cheese sauce, tomatoes, mushrooms, and chili powder. Stir in meat mixture.

3. Cover; cook on low-heat setting for 8 to 10 hours or on high-heat setting for 4 to 5 hours. Stir in macaroni. Cover and cook 15 minutes more.

Nutrition Facts per serving: 335 calories, 20 g total fat, 69 mg cholesterol, 1,179 mg sodium, 20 g carbohydrate, 19 g protein.

1 pound ground beef

½ cup chopped onion

1 16-ounce jar process cheese sauce

1 14½-ounce can Mexican-style stewed tomatoes, undrained

1 2½-ounce jar sliced mushrooms, drained

2 teaspoons chili powder

2 cups cooked wagon wheel or elbow macaroni

Sloppy Joes

It may be messy eating, but it sure does taste good! Make this classic sandwich with ground pork or ground turkey rather than beef for a change of pace.

Prep: 20 minutes **Cook:** 6 hours on low or 3 hours on high **Makes:** 8 servings

1½ pounds ground beef

1 cup chopped onion

2 cloves garlic, minced

¾ cup ketchup

½ cup chopped green
sweet pepper

½ cup chopped celery

¼ cup water

1 to 2 tablespoons
packed brown sugar

2 tablespoon yellow mustard

2 tablespoons vinegar

2 tablespoons Worcestershire
sauce

1½ teaspoons chili powder

8 hamburger buns,
split and toasted

1. In a large skillet cook ground beef, onion, and garlic until meat is brown and onion is tender. Drain off fat.

2. Meanwhile, in a 3½- or 4-quart slow cooker combine ketchup, sweet pepper, celery, water, brown sugar, mustard, vinegar, Worcestershire sauce, and chili powder. Stir in meat.

3. Cover; cook on low-heat setting for 6 to 8 hours or on high-heat setting for 3 to 4 hours. Spoon into toasted buns.

Nutrition Facts per serving: 340 calories, 13 g total fat, 53 mg cholesterol, 690 mg sodium, 35 g carbohydrate, 21 g protein.

Hot-and-Spicy Sloppy Joes

Hot-style tomato juice and jalapeño peppers give new life to these saucy sandwiches.

Prep: 20 minutes **Cook:** 10 hours on low or 3 hours on high **Makes:** 8 servings

1. In a large skillet cook ground beef, onion, and garlic until meat is brown and onion is tender. Drain off fat.

2. Meanwhile, in a 3 ½ or 4-quart slow cooker combine tomato juice, ketchup, water, brown sugar, jalapeño peppers, (if desired) mustard, chili powder, and Worcestershire sauce. Stir in meat mixture. Cover; cook on low-heat setting for 10 to 12 hours or high-heat setting for 3 to 5 hours. Toast buns; spoon meat mixture into buns and sprinkle with cheese.

For 5- or 6-quart slow cooker: Double all ingredients; prepare as above. Makes 16 servings.

Nutrition Facts per serving: 361 calories, 16 g total fat, 60 mg cholesterol, 606 mg sodium, 33 g carbohydrate, 21 g protein.

1½ pounds ground beef
1 large onion, chopped (1 cup)
1 clove garlic, minced
1 6-ounce can hot-style tomato juice or vegetable juice cocktail
½ cup ketchup
½ cup water
2 tablespoons packed brown sugar
2 tablespoons chopped canned Jalapeño peppers (optional)
1 tablespoon yellow mustard
2 teaspoons chili powder
1 teaspoon Worcestershire sauce
8 hamburger buns
Shredded cheddar cheese

New England Boiled Dinner

A creamy horseradish sour cream sauce freshens up this hearty American classic.

Prep: 20 minutes **Cook:** 11 hours on low plus 30 minutes on high or 6 hours on high **Makes:** 8 servings

½ cup mayonnaise
    or salad dressing
½ cup dairy sour cream
2 tablespoons horseradish
    mustard
2 teaspoons snipped
    fresh chives
6 medium potatoes, peeled
    and quartered (about
    2 pounds)
6 medium carrots,
    cut in 2-inch lengths
1 large onion, quartered
3 cloves garlic, minced
1 3- to 3½-pound
    corned beef brisket
2 teaspoons dillseeds
1 teaspoon dried rosemary,
    crushed
½ teaspoon salt
2 14-ounce cans beef broth
1 small head cabbage,
    cut into 8 wedges

1. In a small bowl stir together mayonnaise, sour cream, horseradish mustard, and chives. Cover; chill until serving time or up to 24 hours.

2. In a 5- or 6-quart slow cooker place potatoes, carrots, onion, and garlic. Top with corned beef brisket; discard seasoning packet if present. Sprinkle with dillseeds, rosemary, and salt. Pour beef broth over meat.

3. Cover; cook on low-heat setting for 11 to 12 hours or on high-heat setting for 5½ to 6 hours.

4. If using low-heat setting, turn to high-heat setting. Add cabbage wedges. Cover; cook for 30 minutes more. Remove meat from cooker. Thinly slice meat across the grain. Remove vegetables with a slotted spoon and serve with meat. Serve mayonnaise mixture with meat and vegetables.

Nutrition Facts per serving: 540 calories, 35 g total fat, 100 mg cholesterol, 767 mg sodium, 27 g carbohydrate, 30 g protein.

Corned Beef Hash

A warming dinner for those red-flannel days in the fall and winter.

Prep: 10 minutes **Cook:** 4 hours on low or 2 hours on high **Makes:** 6 to 8 servings

1. In a 3½-, 4-, or 5-quart slow cooker combine hash brown potatoes, corned beef, onion, broth, and pepper.

2. Cover; cook on low-heat setting for 4 to 6 hours or on high-heat setting for 2 to 3 hours.

Nutrition Facts per serving: **393 calories, 20 g total fat, 98 mg cholesterol, 1,303 mg sodium, 30 g carbohydrate, 23 g protein.**

Roast Beef Hash: Substitute cooked roast beef for the corned beef, beef broth for the chicken broth, and add ¼ teaspoon salt.

1 32-ounce package
   frozen hash brown potatoes
4 cups finely chopped
   cooked corned beef
1 cup chopped onion
1 cup chicken broth
½ teaspoon ground black
   pepper

Cheesy Scalloped Potatoes and Ham

This old-fashioned favorite used to require lots of potato-peeling and a stint in the oven.

This easy version takes advantage of prepared potatoes and the convenience of a slow cooker.

Prep: 10 minutes **Cook:** 7 hours on low or 3½ hours on high **Makes:** 4 servings

1 24-ounce package frozen hash brown potatoes with onion and peppers

2 cups diced fully cooked ham (10-ounces)

1 2-ounce jar diced pimiento, drained

1 tablespoon snipped fresh parsley

¼ teaspoon ground black pepper

1 11-ounce can condensed cheddar cheese soup

¾ cup milk

1. In a 3½-, 4-, or 5-quart slow cooker combine hash brown potatoes, ham, pimiento, parsley, and pepper.

2. In a medium bowl combine the soup and milk; pour over the potato mixture in the slow cooker.

3. Cover; cook on low-heat setting for 7 to 9 hours or on high-heat setting for 3½ to 4 hours. Stir before serving.

Nutrition Facts per serving: 470 calories, 24 g total fat, 43 mg cholesterol, 1,454 mg sodium, 42 g carbohydrate, 24 g protein.

Bavarian Pork Roast

For a truly German-style meal, serve this well-seasoned pork and tangy gravy with Bavarian-style sauerkraut, dark rye bread, and a mug of cold beer.

Prep: 25 minutes **Cook:** 8 hours on low or 4 hours on high **Makes:** 6 servings

1. Trim fat from roast. If necessary, cut roast to fit into a 3½-, 4-, 5-, or 6-quart slow cooker. Combine caraway seeds, marjoram, salt, and pepper. Rub all over roast.

2. In a large skillet brown pork roast on all sides in hot oil. Drain off fat. Place meat in slow cooker. Add the water to skillet; bring to a gentle boil over medium heat, stirring to loosen brown bits in bottom of skillet. Pour skillet juices and vinegar into slow cooker.

3. Cover; cook on low-heat setting for 8 to 10 hours or on high-heat setting for 4 to 5 hours. Remove meat from cooker; keep warm.

4. For gravy, skim fat from juices; measure 1¼ cups juices (add water, if necessary). Pour juices into a saucepan; bring to boiling. Combine sour cream and cornstarch. Stir into juices. Cook and stir over medium heat until thickened and bubbly. Cook and stir 2 minutes more. Slice meat and serve with gravy.

Nutrition Facts per serving: 262 calories, 15 g total fat, 73 mg cholesterol, 365 mg sodium, 4 g carbohydrate, 26 g protein.

1 1½- to 2-pound boneless pork shoulder roast
2 teaspoons caraway seeds
1 teaspoon dried marjoram, crushed
¾ teaspoon salt
½ teaspoon ground black pepper
1 tablespoon olive oil or cooking oil
½ cup water
2 tablespoons white wine vinegar
1 8-ounce carton dairy sour cream or plain yogurt
4 teaspoons cornstarch

Cranberry Pork Roast

In this slow-simmered pork dish, a ruby-color fruit sauce provides good nutrition and great taste.

Prep: 20 minutes **Cook:** 5½ hours on low **Makes:** 12 servings

4 medium potatoes,
   peeled and cubed
1 3-pound boneless pork
   top loin roast
1 16-ounce can whole
   cranberry sauce
1 15-ounce can apricot
   halves, drained
1 medium onion, chopped
½ cup snipped dried apricots
2 tablespoons sugar
1 teaspoon dry mustard
¼ teaspoon ground red pepper
1 tablespoon cornstarch
1 tablespoon cold water

1. Place potatoes in bottom of a 5- or 6-quart slow cooker. Place meat on potatoes; set aside. In a blender container or food processor bowl combine cranberry sauce, drained apricots, onion, dried apricots, sugar, mustard, and red pepper. Cover and blend or process until nearly smooth.

2. Pour fruit mixture over pork. Cover; cook on low-heat setting for 5½ to 6½ hours. Remove roast and potatoes to platter. Cover and keep warm.

3. For sauce, transfer cooking juices from cooker to a 4-cup glass measure. Skim off fat. Measure 2 cups juices; discard remaining juices. Pour juices into a medium saucepan. Stir together cornstarch and the water. Add to saucepan, stirring to combine. Cook and stir over medium heat until thickened and bubbly; cook and stir 2 minutes more. Slice roast. Serve sauce with potatoes and roast.

Nutrition Facts per serving : 307 calories, 6 g total fat, 67 mg cholesterol, 75 mg sodium, 36 g carbohydrate, 26 g protein.

Cuban Pork

Serve these spice-and-citrus-sauced wraps with a tropical fruit salad.

Prep: 25 minutes **Marinate:** 6 hours **Cook:** 10 hours on low or 5 hours on high **Makes:** 8 to 10 servings

---

1. For the marinade, in a small bowl combine fruit juices, water, garlic, oregano, cumin, salt, pepper, and the bay leaves. Trim fat from meat*. Pierce pork roast in several places with a large fork. Place in a plastic bag set in a deep bowl or a baking dish; add marinade. Close bag and turn to coat. Marinate, covered, in the refrigerator for 6 to 24 hours, turning occasionally.

2. In a 3½-, 4, or 5-quart slow cooker, place onion. Top with meat and marinade mixture.

3. Cover; cook on low-heat setting for 10 to 12 hours or on high-heat setting for 5 to 6 hours.

4. To serve, remove meat from cooker; cool slightly. Skim fat from juices. Shred meat; remove onions from juices with a slotted spoon and add to meat. Discard bay leaves. Serve meat in flour tortillas with small bowls of the hot juices.

Trimming meat: If meat has netting, peel back netting to trim.

Nutrition Facts per serving: 385 calories, 13 g total fat, 110 mg cholesterol, 465 mg sodium, 27 g carbohydrate, 37 g protein.

½ cup lime juice
¼ cup grapefruit juice
¼ cup water
3 cloves garlic, minced
1 teaspoon dried oregano, crushed
½ teaspoon ground cumin
½ teaspoon salt
¼ teaspoon ground black pepper
2 bay leaves
1 3- to 4-pound boneless pork shoulder roast
1 cup sliced onion
Flour tortillas

Pork Roast with Cherries

Cherries pair perfectly with pork, but you also can use coarsely chopped cranberries, apricots, golden raisins, or dried mixed fruit.

Prep: 20 minutes **Cook:** 7 hours on low or 3½ hours on high **Makes:** 6 to 8 servings

1 2- to 2½-pound boneless pork shoulder roast

2 tablespoons cooking oil

1 tablespoon quick-cooking tapioca

1 tablespoon snipped fresh thyme or 1 teaspoon dried thyme, crushed

½ teaspoon ground black pepper

1 medium onion, sliced

1 cup dried cherries

½ cup apple juice or apple cider

3 to 4 cups hot cooked rice or noodles

1. Trim fat from meat. If necessary, cut roast to fit into a 3½-, 4-, 5-, or 6-quart slow cooker. In a large skillet brown meat on all sides in hot oil. Drain off fat.

2. Transfer meat to cooker. Sprinkle tapioca, dried thyme (if using), and pepper over meat. Add onion and dried cherries. Pour apple juice over all.

3. Cover; cook on low-heat setting for 7 to 9 hours or on high-heat setting for 3½ to 4½ hours. Transfer meat to serving platter; cover to keep warm.

4. For sauce, skim fat from cooking juices. If using, stir fresh thyme into juices. Serve meat and cooking juices with hot cooked rice or noodles.

Nutrition Facts per serving: 460 calories, 18 g total fat, 99 mg cholesterol, 80 mg sodium, 43 g carbohydrate, 29 g protein.

Pork Hocks and Black-Eyed Peas

Southerners swear by a feast of black-eyed peas on New Year's Day to give them good luck throughout the year. Serve 'em up with warm corn bread.

Prep: 25 minutes **Stand:** 1 hour 10 minutes **Cook:** 8 hours on low or 4 hours on high **Stand:** 10 minutes **Makes:** 6 servings

---

1. Rinse black-eyed peas; place in a large saucepan. Add enough water to cover peas by 2 inches. Bring to boiling; reduce heat. Simmer, uncovered, for 10 minutes. Remove from heat. Cover; let stand for 1 hour. Drain and rinse peas.

2. In a 3½-, 4-, or 5-quart slow cooker combine the black-eyed peas, pork hocks, broth, sweet pepper, onion, celery, bay leaves, and red pepper.

3. Cover; cook on low-heat setting for 8 to 10 hours or on high-heat setting for 4 to 5 hours. Add okra. Cover; let stand for 10 minutes or until okra is tender. Remove pork hocks. When cool enough to handle, cut meat off bones; cut meat into bite-size pieces. Discard bones and bay leaves. To serve, stir meat into black-eyed pea mixture.

Nutrition Facts per serving: **191 calories, 3 g total fat, 14 mg cholesterol, 763 mg sodium, 28 g carbohydrate, 15 g protein.**

1½ cups dry black-eyed peas (8 ounces)

4 small smoked pork hocks (1½ pounds)

4 cups reduced-sodium chicken broth

1 medium green sweet pepper, chopped (¾ cup)

1 medium onion, chopped (¾ cup)

1 stalk celery, chopped (½ cup)

2 bay leaves

¼ teaspoon ground red pepper

2 cups sliced okra or one 10-ounce package frozen whole okra, thawed and cut into ½-inch slices

Barbecue-Style Pork Sandwiches

Coleslaw is a great condiment for these zippy barbecued sandwiches—piled right on top of the meat—or served alongside as an accompaniment.

Prep: 15 minutes **Cook:** 10 hours on low or 5 hours on high **Makes:** 6 servings

2 large green sweet peppers,
  cut into strips (2½ cups)
1 large onion, thinly sliced
  and separated into rings
  (1 cup)
2 tablespoons quick-cooking
  tapioca
1 2½- to 3-pound pork
  shoulder roast
1 10¾-ounce can condensed
  tomato soup
2 tablespoons steak sauce
3 to 4 teaspoons chili powder
½ teaspoon sugar
¼ teaspoon garlic powder
¼ teaspoon ground black
  pepper
  Several dashes bottled
  hot pepper sauce
6 kaiser rolls, split
  Coleslaw, drained (optional)

1. In a 3½-, 4-, 5-, or 6-quart slow cooker combine sweet pepper strips and onion rings. Sprinkle tapioca over vegetables. Trim fat from roast. If necessary, cut roast to fit into cooker. Place roast on top of vegetables.

2. For barbecue sauce, in a medium bowl combine tomato soup, steak sauce, chili powder, sugar, garlic powder, pepper, and hot pepper sauce. Pour over roast.

3. Cover; cook on low-heat setting for 10 to 12 hours or on high-heat setting for 5 to 6 hours. Remove roast from cooker and thinly slice or shred meat. Skim fat from sauce.

4. Serve meat on kaiser rolls; top with barbecue sauce and, if desired, coleslaw.

Nutrition Facts per serving: **511 calories, 14 g total fat, 122 mg cholesterol, 867 mg sodium, 49 g carbohydrate, 45 g protein.**

Curried Pork and Apples

Tart Granny Smith apples are a great choice to make this aromatic curry.

Prep: 25 minutes **Cook:** 10 hours on low or 5 hours on high **Makes:** 6 servings

1. Trim fat from roast; cut pork into 1-inch cubes. In a large skillet brown pork, half at a time, in hot oil. Transfer pork to a 3½- or 4-quart slow cooker; sprinkle with tapioca. Add water, apples, onion, raisins, curry, bouillon granules, and paprika.

2. Cover; cook on low-heat setting for 10 to 12 hours or on high-heat setting for 5 to 6 hours. Serve over rice.

For 5- or 6-quart slow cooker: Use one 3-pound boneless pork shoulder roast, 3 tablespoons cooking oil, ⅓ cup quick-cooking tapioca, 3 cups water, 3 medium cooking apples, cored and quartered, 1⅓ cups chopped onion, ⅔ cup raisins, 3 tablespoons curry powder, 4 teaspoons instant chicken bouillon granules, ½ teaspoon paprika, and hot cooked rice. Prepare as above. Makes 8 to 10 servings.

Nutrition Facts per serving: 461 calories, 14 g total fat, 98 mg cholesterol, 562 mg sodium, 49 g carbohydrate, 34 g protein.

1 2-pound boneless pork
   shoulder roast
2 tablespoons cooking oil
¼ cup quick-cooking tapioca
2 cups water
2 medium cooking apples,
   cored and cut into quarters
1 cup chopped onion
½ cup raisins
2 tablespoons curry powder
1 tablespoon instant chicken
   bouillon granules
½ teaspoon paprika
   Hot cooked rice

Fennel Pork Roast and Vegetables

Fresh fennel is at its peak from September through April. Look for firm, smooth bulbs without cracks and brown spots. Use the bright green fennel leaves as a garnish.

Prep: 25 minutes **Cook:** 8 hours on low or 4 hours on high **Makes:** 6 to 8 servings

---

1 2- to 2½-pound boneless
    pork shoulder roast
1 teaspoon fennel seeds,
    crushed
½ teaspoon garlic powder
½ teaspoon dried oregano,
    crushed
¼ teaspoon ground black
    pepper
2 tablespoons cooking oil
1½ pounds small red potatoes,
    halved
1 large fennel bulb, trimmed
    and cut into 1-inch pieces
2 cups cold water
2 teaspoons instant chicken
    bouillon granules
¼ cup all-purpose flour
    Salt and ground black
    pepper

1. Trim fat from meat. In a small bowl combine fennel seeds, garlic powder, oregano, and ¼ teaspoon pepper. Rub about 1 teaspoon of the seasoning mixture evenly over roast. In a Dutch oven brown meat on all sides in hot oil. Drain off fat.

2. Place potatoes and fennel in bottom of a 3½- or 4-quart slow cooker. Sprinkle with remaining seasoning mixture. Stir together the 1½ cups of the water and bouillon granules; add to cooker. Cut meat, if necessary, to fit into the slow cooker. Place roast on top of vegetable mixture.

3. Cover; cook on low-heat setting for 8 to 10 hours or on high-heat setting for 4 to 5 hours.

4. For gravy, skim fat from juices. Measure 1½ cups juices into a medium saucepan. Stir the remaining ½ cup cold water into the flour; stir into reserved juices in saucepan. Cook and stir until thickened and bubbly. Cook and stir 1 minute more. Season to taste with salt and pepper. Pass gravy with meat.

Nutrition Facts per serving: 439 calories, 20 g total fat, 99 mg cholesterol, 451 mg sodium, 33 g carbohydrate, 30 g protein.

Orange-Herbed Pork Roast

This orange-sauced pork roast goes great with parslied new potatoes and steamed baby carrots and sugar snap peas.

Prep: 25 minutes **Cook:** 8 hours on low or 4 hours on high **Makes:** 8 servings

1. Trim fat from pork roast. If necessary, cut roast to fit into slow cooker. In a small bowl combine garlic powder, ginger, thyme, and the ¼ teaspoon pepper. Rub spice mixture over entire surface of meat with fingers. In a large skillet brown roast on all sides in hot oil. Drain.

2. Transfer meat to a 3½-, 4-, or 5-quart slow cooker. Combine chicken broth, sugar, lemon juice, soy sauce, and orange peel; pour over roast.

3. Cover; cook on low-heat setting for 8 to 10 hours or on high-heat setting for 4 to 5 hours.

4. Transfer roast to a serving platter; keep warm. For sauce, pour juices into glass measure. Skim fat. If necessary, add water to equal 2 cups. Transfer to saucepan. Combine cornstarch and orange juice; stir into juices in saucepan. Cook and stir until thickened and bubbly. Cook and stir 2 minutes more. If desired, season to taste. Pass sauce with meat.

Nutrition Facts per serving: **197 calories, 6 g total fat, 78 mg cholesterol, 224 mg sodium, 8 g carbohydrate, 29 g protein.**

1 **2½- to 3-pound pork sirloin roast**
½ **teaspoon garlic powder**
½ **teaspoon ground ginger**
½ **teaspoon dried thyme, crushed**
¼ **teaspoon ground black pepper**
1 **tablespoon cooking oil**
1 **cup chicken broth**
2 **tablespoons sugar**
2 **tablespoons lemon juice**
2 **teaspoons soy sauce**
1½ **teaspoons finely shredded orange peel**
3 **tablespoons cornstarch**
½ **cup orange juice**
   Salt and ground black pepper (optional)

Apricot-Glazed Pork Roast

Cook some rice to serve as a side and to soak up the sweet and savory mustard-spiked apricot sauce.

Prep: 15 minutes **Cook:** 10 hours on low or 5 hours on high **Makes:** 6 to 8 servings

1 3- to 3½-pound boneless
  pork shoulder roast
1 18-ounce jar apricot
  preserves
¼ cup chicken broth
2 tablespoons Dijon-style
  mustard
1 large onion, chopped
  (1 cup)

1. Trim fat from roast. If necessary, cut roast to fit into a 3½-, 4-, 5-, or 6-quart slow cooker. Place meat in cooker. Combine preserves, broth, mustard, and onion; pour over meat.

2. Cover; cook on low-heat setting for 10 to 12 hours or on high-heat setting for 5 to 6 hours. Transfer meat to a serving plate. Skim off fat from sauce. Spoon some of the sauce over meat; discard any remaining sauce.

Nutrition Facts per serving: **456 calories, 10 g total fat, 93 mg cholesterol, 184 mg sodium, 61 g carbohydrate, 29 g protein.**

Lemon Pork and Couscous

Flavored with fresh basil and shallots, this one-dish dinner is well-suited to weeknight entertaining or for weekend celebrations when you want to be part of the party instead of stuck in the kitchen.

Prep: 30 minutes **Cook:** 7 hours on low plus 5 minutes on high or 3 hours and 35 minutes on high **Makes:** 6 servings

1. Trim fat from pork. Cut pork into 1-inch pieces. Combine flour and pepper in a plastic bag. Add pork, close bag, and shake until pork is coated with flour. In a large skillet brown half of the meat in 1 tablespoon of the oil about 5 minutes, turning to brown evenly. Remove from skillet. Brown remaining pork in remaining 1 tablespoon oil about 5 minutes, turning to brown evenly.

2. In a 3½-, 4-, 5-, or 6-quart slow cooker place carrots, parsnips, shallots, lemon, and basil. Place pork on top of vegetables. Pour broth over all.

3. Cover; cook on low-heat setting for 7 to 8 hours or on high-heat setting for 3½ to 4 hours. Discard lemon pieces.

4. Use a slotted spoon to remove pork and vegetables to a serving dish, reserving juices; cover meat and keep warm. Measure 1¾ cups of the cooking juices and return to slow cooker. Discard remaining cooking liquid. If using low-heat setting, turn to high-heat setting. Stir in couscous. Cover; cook for 5 minutes more on high-heat setting. Fluff couscous with a fork. Serve pork and vegetables over couscous.

Nutrition Facts per serving: 511 calories, 16 g total fat, 101 mg cholesterol, 368 mg sodium, 53 g carbohydrate, 38 g protein.

2 pounds boneless
  pork shoulder
¼ cup all-purpose flour
½ teaspoon ground black
  pepper
2 tablespoons cooking oil
1 1-pound package peeled baby
  carrots
8 ounces parsnips, cut into
  ½-inch slices
2 medium shallots, sliced
1 lemon, quartered
¼ cup thinly sliced fresh basil
1 14½-ounce can
  chicken broth
1⅓ cups quick-cooking couscous

Pineapple-Ginger Pork

You have to stand over a stir-fry and, well, stir. This Chinese-inspired dish cooks without watching or stirring and costs a lot less than take-out.

Prep: 30 minutes **Cook:** 6 hours on low plus 10 minutes on high or 3 hours and 10 minutes on high **Makes:** 6 to 8 servings

2 pounds boneless
    pork shoulder
2 tablespoons cooking oil
¾ cup chicken broth
3 tablespoons quick-cooking
    tapioca
3 tablespoons low-sodium
    soy sauce
3 tablespoons oyster sauce
    (optional)
1 teaspoon grated
    fresh ginger
1 15¼-ounce can pineapple
    chunks (juice pack)
4 medium carrots, cut into
    ½-inch slices (2 cups)
1 large onion, cut into
    1-inch pieces
1 8-ounce can sliced water
    chestnuts, drained
1½ cups fresh snow pea pods
    or one 6-ounce package
    frozen pea pods
3 cups hot cooked rice

1. Trim fat from pork. Cut pork into 1-inch pieces. In a large skillet brown half of the pork at a time in hot oil. Drain off fat.

2. In a 3½- or 4-quart slow cooker combine chicken broth, tapioca, soy sauce, oyster sauce (if using), and ginger. Drain pineapple, reserving juice. Stir juice into broth mixture; cover and chill pineapple chunks. Add carrots, onion, and water chestnuts to cooker. Add pork.

3. Cover; cook on low-heat setting for 6 to 8 hours or on high-heat setting for 3 to 4 hours.

4. If using low-heat setting, turn to high-heat setting. Stir pineapple chunks and the snow peas into cooker. Cover; cook 10 to 15 minutes more on high-heat setting or until peas are crisp-tender. Serve over rice.

For a 5- to 6-quart cooker: Recipe may be doubled.

Nutrition Facts per serving: 402 calories, 11 g total fat, 62 mg cholesterol, 477 mg sodium, 51 g carbohydrate, 23 g protein.

North Carolina Pork Barbecue

Barbecue styles vary greatly from region to region. Some—like this spicy North Carolina-style pork—don't call for even a smidgen of ketchup or molasses.

Prep: 10 minutes **Cook:** 10 hours on low or 5 hours on high **Makes:** 16 servings

1. In a 4-, 5-, or 6-quart slow cooker place the meat, vinegar, water, sugar, salt, and peppers.

2. Cover; cook on low-heat setting 10 to 12 hours or high-heat setting 5 to 6 hours. Remove meat from cooker; cool slightly. Remove meat from bone. Shred or chop the meat. Stir in as much of the cooking liquid as desired to moisten meat. If desired, serve on rolls.

Nutrition Facts per serving: **183 calories, 5 g total fat, 44 mg cholesterol, 284 mg sodium, 17 g carbohydrate, 16 g protein.**

1 4- to 5-pound pork shoulder
   roast or Boston butt
1 cup white vinegar
½ cup water
2 tablespoons sugar
½ teaspoon salt
½ teaspoon crushed red pepper
¼ teaspoon ground black
   pepper
8 kaiser rolls, split and toasted
   (optional)

Plum-Sauced Pork Wraps

Make your own moo-shu! Crisp Chinese cabbage is a great companion for the sweet, spicy meat.

Prep: 15 minutes **Cook:** 8 hours on low or 4 hours on high **Makes:** 8 servings

1 2½- to 3-pound boneless
   pork shoulder roast
1 teaspoon ground ginger
½ teaspoon garlic powder
1 16-ounce package frozen
   stir-fry vegetables
1 8½-ounce jar plum or hoisin
   sauce
½ cup chicken broth
2 cups shredded chinese
   cabbage (napa
   or bok choy)
8 10-inch flour tortillas,
   warmed

1. Remove string from meat, if present. Trim fat from pork roast. If necessary, cut roast to fit into a 3½- or 4-quart slow cooker. Sprinkle meat with ginger and garlic powder and rub into meat with fingers.

2. Transfer meat to slow cooker. Add vegetables, half of the plum sauce, and the broth.

3. Cover; cook on low-heat setting for 8 to 10 hours or on high-heat setting for 4 to 5 hours.

4. Remove meat from cooker. Using 2 forks, shred meat and place in a large bowl. Remove vegetables with a slotted spoon and add to pork in bowl (discard liquid). Add remaining plum sauce and stir to combine. Place shredded cabbage and pork and vegetable mixture on centers of tortillas. Fold bottom edges of warmed tortillas up and over filling. Fold opposite sides in, just until they meet. Roll up from the bottom. Secure with wooden toothpicks.

Nutrition Facts per serving: 393 calories, 13 g total fat, 92 mg cholesterol, 377 mg sodium, 35 g carbohydrate, 34 g protein.

Jamaican Jerk Pork Sandwiches

Jerk seasoning—a savory blend of chiles, thyme, cinnamon, ginger, allspice, and cloves—flavors these sandwiches. Serve them with sweet potato chips.

Prep: 30 minutes **Cook:** 8 hours on low or 4 hours on high **Makes:** 6 to 8 servings

1. Trim fat from meat. Rub jerk seasoning evenly over roast. Place meat in a 3½-or 4-quart slow cooker, sprinkle with thyme, and pour water over roast.

2. Cover; cook on low-heat setting for 8 to 10 hours or on high-heat setting for 4 to 5 hours. Remove meat from cooker, reserving juices. Shred meat, discarding any fat. Skim fat from juices. Add enough of the juices to moisten meat (about ½ cup). Stir lime juice into meat.

3. To serve, use a slotted spoon to place pork mixture onto roll bottoms. If desired, layer with lettuce leaves, sweet pepper rings, and mango slices. Spoon Lime Mayo onto each sandwich; cover with roll tops.

Nutrition Facts per serving: 430 calories, 21 g total fat, 74 mg cholesterol, 609 mg sodium, 34 g carbohydrate, 26 g protein.

Lime Mayo: In a bowl stir together ½ cup light mayonnaise dressing or regular mayonnaise, ¼ cup finely chopped red onion, ¼ teaspoon finely shredded lime peel, 1 tablespoon lime juice, and 1 clove garlic, minced. Cover; chill until ready to serve.

1 1½-to 2-pound boneless
 pork shoulder roast
1 tablespoon Jamaican jerk
 seasoning
¼ teaspoon dried thyme,
 crushed
1 cup water
1 tablespoon lime juice
6 to 8 kaiser rolls, split
 and toasted
6 to 8 lettuce leaves (optional)
6 thinly sliced red
 or green sweet pepper rings
 (optional)
1 medium mango, peeled
 and thinly sliced (optional)
1 recipe Lime Mayo

Barbecue-Style Ribs

Love ribs but don't want to stand over a hot grill? Let meaty pork ribs "barbecue" on your countertop all day. Shred leftover meat for sandwiches.

Prep: 5 minutes **Cook:** 10 hours on low or 5 hours on high **Broil:** 10 minutes **Makes:** 4 servings

3 to 3½ pounds pork
    country-style ribs,
    cut crosswise in half
    and cut into 2-rib portions
1 cup ketchup
½ cup finely chopped onion
¼ cup packed brown sugar
1 tablespoon Worcestershire
    sauce
½ teaspoon chili powder
½ teaspoon Liquid Smoke
¼ teaspoon garlic powder
¼ teaspoon bottled hot
    pepper sauce

1. Preheat broiler. Place ribs on the unheated rack of a broiler pan. Broil 6 inches from the heat until brown, about 10 minutes, turning once. Transfer ribs to a 3½- or 4-quart slow cooker.

2. In a small bowl combine ketchup, onion, brown sugar, Worcestershire sauce, chili powder, Liquid Smoke, garlic powder, and hot pepper sauce. Pour sauce over ribs, turning to coat.

3. Cover; cook on low-heat setting for 10 to 12 hours or on high-heat setting for 5 to 6 hours.

4. Transfer ribs to a platter. If desired, skim fat from surface of sauce; pour sauce into a medium saucepan. Simmer sauce until reduced and thickened. Pass sauce with ribs.

Nutrition Facts per serving: 940 calories, 51 g total fat, 316 mg cholesterol, 1,115 mg sodium, 33 g carbohydrate, 86 g protein.

Asian-Style Ribs

Three kinds of pepper—black, red, and hot pepper sauce—give these Chinese-style ribs their kick.

Prep: 15 minutes **Cook:** 8 hours on low or 4 hours on high **Makes:** 6 servings

1. Place ribs in a 3½- or 4-quart slow cooker, cutting as necessary to fit.

2. For sauce, in a small bowl combine green onion, soy sauce, molasses, hoisin sauce, brown sugar, vinegar, sesame oil, lemon juice, hot pepper sauce, ginger, garlic powder, chili powder, red pepper, and black pepper. Pour the sauce over the ribs in cooker, turning to coat.

3. Cover; cook on low-heat setting for 8 to 10 hours or on high-heat setting for 4 to 5 hours. Transfer ribs to serving platter. Strain sauce; skim off fat. Serve sauce over ribs and rice.

Nutrition Facts per serving: 532 calories, 31 g total fat, 69 mg cholesterol, 511 mg sodium, 32 g carbohydrate, 30 g protein.

Sweet 'n' Peppery Country-Style Rib Sandwiches: Prepare the ribs as directed above, except omit the hot cooked rice. Remove the cooked meat from the bones. Using 2 forks, pull meat apart into shreds. To serve, add meat to split and toasted, large sesame buns or kaiser rolls. Serve the strained sauce on the side. Makes 8 to 10 sandwiches.

3½ pounds pork
   country-style ribs
6 green onions, chopped
¼ cup reduced-sodium
   soy sauce
¼ cup molasses
2 tablespoons hoisin sauce
2 tablespoons packed
   brown sugar
2 tablespoons white
   wine vinegar
2 teaspoons toasted
   sesame oil
2 teaspoons lemon juice
½ teaspoon bottled
   hot pepper sauce
½ teaspoon ground ginger
½ teaspoon garlic powder
½ teaspoon chili powder
¼ teaspoon ground red pepper
¼ teaspoon ground
   black pepper
2 cups hot cooked rice

Country Ribs

Serve these meaty ribs with baked beans, coleslaw, and cherry-peach cobbler.

Prep: 10 minutes **Cook:** 10 hours on low or 5 hours on high **Makes:** 4 to 6 servings

1 large onion, sliced and
   separated into rings
2½ to 3 pounds pork
   country-style ribs
1½ cups vegetable
   juice cocktail
½ of a 6-ounce can tomato
   paste (⅓ cup)
¼ cup molasses
3 tablespoons vinegar
1 teaspoon dry mustard
¼ teaspoon salt
¼ teaspoon ground black
   pepper
⅛ teaspoon dried thyme,
   crushed
⅛ teaspoon dried rosemary,
   crushed

1. In a 3½-, 4-, 5-, or 6-quart slow cooker place onion rings. Place ribs on top of onion. Combine vegetable juice cocktail, tomato paste, molasses, vinegar, dry mustard, salt, pepper, thyme, and rosemary. Reserve 1 cup for sauce; cover and refrigerate. Pour remaining mixture over ribs. Cover; cook on low-heat setting for 10 to 12 hours or on high-heat setting for 5 to 6 hours.

2. For sauce, in a small saucepan simmer reserved mixture, uncovered, for 10 minutes. Drain ribs; discard cooking liquid. Serve sauce with ribs.

Nutrition Facts per serving: 355 calories, 13 g total fat, 101 mg cholesterol, 519 mg sodium, 26 g carbohydrate, 33 g protein.

Aloha Pork Steaks

These island-style steaks get their name from a sweet-and-sour pineapple sauce.

Prep: 15 minutes **Cook:** 6 hours on low or 3 hours on high **Makes:** 4 servings

1. In a large skillet brown pork steaks on both sides in hot oil. Drain off fat. Transfer steaks to a 3½- or 4 quart slow cooker.

2. In a bowl combine pineapple, sweet pepper, water, brown sugar, tapioca, ketchup, soy sauce, and dry mustard; pour over steaks.

3. Cover; cook on low-heat setting for 6 to 8 hours or on high-heat setting for 3 to 4 hours. Skim fat from sauce. Serve over hot cooked rice.

Nutrition Facts per serving: **482 calories, 16 g total fat, 93 mg cholesterol, 356 mg sodium, 57 g carbohydrate, 27 g protein.**

4 pork shoulder steaks,
    cut ½-inch thick
2 teaspoons cooking oil
1 8-ounce can crushed
    pineapple, undrained
½ cup chopped green
    sweet pepper
½ cup water
⅓ cup packed brown sugar
2 tablespoons quick-cooking
    tapioca
2 tablespoons ketchup
2 teaspoons soy sauce
½ teaspoon dry mustard
2 cups hot cooked rice

Pork Chops with Apples and Sauerkraut

If you like sauerkraut a little less lip-puckering, rinse and drain it in a colander before placing it in the slow cooker.

Prep: 20 minutes **Cook:** 6 hours on low or 3 hours on high **Makes:** 4 servings

4 pork sirloin chops,
   cut ¾ inch thick
   (about 1½ pounds)
1 tablespoon cooking oil
2 medium potatoes,
   cut into ¼-inch slices
2 medium carrots,
   cut into ½-inch pieces
1 medium onion, thinly sliced
1 16-ounce can sauerkraut,
   drained
2 small cooking apples,
   cut into ¼-inch slices
½ cup apple cider
   or apple juice
¼ cup ketchup
½ teaspoon caraway seeds
   Snipped fresh parsley
   (optional)

1. In a large skillet brown pork chops on both sides in hot oil.

2. In a 3½- or 4-quart slow cooker place potatoes, carrots, onion, browned pork chops, sauerkraut, and apples. In a bowl combine apple cider, and caraway seeds; pour over apples.

3. Cover; cook on low-heat setting for 6 to 8 hours or on high-heat setting for 3 to 4 hours. If desired, garnish with snipped fresh parsley.

Nutrition Facts per serving: 413 calories, 15 g total fat, 77 mg cholesterol, 934 mg sodium, 43 g carbohydrate, 28 g protein.

Pork Chops and Mustard-Sauced Potatoes

If you can't find ¾-inch-thick chops in the self-serve meat case, ask a butcher to carve a bone-in top loin roast into ¾-inch slices.

Prep: 20 minutes **Cook:** 7 hours on low or 3½ hours on high **Makes:** 6 servings

---

1. In a large skillet brown pork chops on both sides, half at a time, in hot oil. Drain off fat.

2. In a large mixing bowl combine soup, wine, mustard, thyme, garlic, and pepper. Add potatoes and onion, stirring to coat. Transfer to a 3½- or 4-quart slow cooker. Place browned chops on top of potatoes.

3. Cover; cook on low-heat setting for 7 to 8 hours or on high-heat setting for 3½ hours.

Nutrition Facts per serving: **335 calories, 11 g total fat, 39 mg cholesterol, 705 mg sodium, 39 g carbohydrate, 17 g protein.**

6 pork loin chops,
  cut ¾ inch thick
1 tablespoon cooking oil
1 10¾-ounce can condensed
  cream of mushroom soup
¼ cup dry white wine
  or chicken broth
¼ cup Dijon-style mustard
1 teaspoon dried thyme,
  crushed
1 clove garlic, minced
¼ teaspoon ground black
  pepper
6 medium potatoes,
  cut into ¼-inch slices
1 medium onion, sliced

Pork Chops with Mushroom Sauce

Serve these mushroom-sauced chops with hot cooked rice, buttered egg noodles, or spaetzle, which can be found in the pasta aisle.

Prep: 20 minutes **Cook:** 10 hours on low or 4½ hours on high **Makes:** 4 servings

4 **pork loin chops,**
   cut ¾ inch thick
1 **tablespoon cooking oil**
1 **small onion, thinly sliced**
1 **10¾-ounce can condensed**
   cream of mushroom soup
¾ **cup dry white wine**
1 **4-ounce can sliced**
   mushrooms, drained
2 **tablespoons quick-cooking**
   tapioca
2 **teaspoons Worcestershire**
   sauce
1 **teaspoon instant beef**
   bouillon granules
¾ **teaspoon dried thyme,**
   crushed
¼ **teaspoon garlic powder**
   Hot cooked rice

1. In a skillet brown chops on both sides in hot oil. In a 3½- or 4-quart slow cooker place onion; add chops. In a bowl combine soup, wine, mushrooms, tapioca, Worcestershire sauce, bouillon granules, thyme, and garlic powder; pour over chops.

2. Cover; cook on low-heat setting for 10 to 12 hours or on high-heat setting for 4½ to 5 hours. Serve over rice.

For 5- or 6-quart slow cooker: Use 6 pork chops, cut in ¾-inch slices. Leave remaining ingredient amounts the same. Prepare as above. Makes 6 servings.

Nutrition Facts per serving: **539 calories, 19 g total fat, 103 mg cholesterol, 979 mg sodium, 37 g carbohydrate, 45 g protein.**

Southwest Pork Chops

In the mood for chili, but only have pork chops in the freezer? Thaw them out, toss them in the slow cooker with a few other ingredients, and warm up with this spicy one-dish meal.

Prep: 15 minutes **Cook:** 5 hours on low plus 30 minutes on high or 3 hours on high **Makes:** 6 servings

1. Trim excess fat from chops. Place chops in the bottom of a 3½- or 4-quart slow cooker. Add chili beans and salsa. Cover; cook on low-heat setting for 5 hours or high-heat setting for 2 ½ hours. If using low heat setting, turn to high-heat setting. Stir in corn. Cover and cook 30 minutes longer. Serve over rice. If desired, sprinkle with cilantro.

2. For all-day cooking: Substitute 8 boneless pork chops (about 2 pounds) for the 6 rib chops. (When cooked this long, chops with bone may leave bony fragments in the cooked mixture.) Cover; cook on low-heat setting for 9½ hours. Turn to high-heat setting Stir in corn. Cover; cook 30 minutes longer. Serve as above.

Note: 2 medium ears of fresh corn equal about 1 cup of whole kernel corn.

Nutrition Facts per serving: **334 calories, 7 g total fat, 77 mg cholesterol, 716 mg sodium, 34 g carbohydrate, 33 g protein.**

- 6 pork rib chops, cut ¾-inch thick (about 2 ½ pounds)
- 1 15-oz. can Mexican-style or Tex-Mex style chili beans
- 1¼ cups bottled salsa
- 1 cup fresh* or frozen whole kernel corn
- 2 cups hot cooked rice
  Snipped fresh cilantro (optional)

Spicy Peanut Pork Chops

Creamy peanut sauce spiked with crushed red pepper cloaks these Thai-style chops. Be sure to use unsweetened coconut milk. Look for it in the Asian foods section of your supermarket.

Prep: 20 minutes **Cook:** 6 hours on low or 3 hours on high **Makes:** 8 servings

---

8 boneless pork chops,
    cut ¾ inch thick
    (about 2 pounds)
1 tablespoon cooking oil
2 cups purchased shredded
    carrots
2 medium onions,
    chopped (1 cup)
1 14-ounce can light
    coconut milk
½ cup chicken broth
½ cup creamy peanut butter
½ teaspoon crushed
    red pepper
6 cups hot cooked basmati
    rice or shredded Chinese
    cabbage (napa)

1. In a large skillet brown pork chops, half at a time, on both sides in hot oil.

2. In a 3½- or 4-quart slow cooker place carrots and onions. In a bowl combine coconut milk, chicken broth, peanut butter, and red pepper; pour over vegetables. Place browned chops on top of vegetables.

3. Cover; cook on low-heat setting for 6 to 8 hours or on high-heat setting for 3 to 4 hours. Serve with rice or cabbage.

Nutrition Facts per serving: **500 calories, 18 g total fat, 62 mg cholesterol, 212 mg sodium, 47 g carbohydrate, 32 g protein.**

Cranberry-Raspberry Sauced Pork Chops

Slices of fresh apricots or plums are stirred in right before serving so they stay juicy and sweet rather than fall apart from overcooking.

Prep: 10 minutes **Cook:** 7 hours on low or 3½ hours on high **Stand:** 5 minutes **Makes:** 6 servings

1. In a 3½- or 4-quart slow cooker place pork chops.

2. For sauce, in a small bowl combine cranberry-orange sauce, raspberry preserves, tapioca, lemon peel, and cardamom. Pour over chops.

3. Cover; cook on low-heat setting for 7 to 8 hours or on high-heat setting for 3½ to 4 hours. Stir in sliced fruit. Cover; let stand 5 minutes. Serve with hot couscous.

Nutrition Facts per serving: 340 calories, 5 g total fat, 27 mg cholesterol, 1,040 mg sodium, 50 g carbohydrate, 23 g protein.

- 6 boneless smoked pork chops (about 1½ pounds)
- 1 cup cranberry-orange sauce
- ½ cup seedless red raspberry preserves
- 1 teaspoon quick-cooking tapioca
- 1 teaspoon finely shredded lemon peel
- ¼ teaspoon ground cardamom
- 3 fresh apricots or plums, pitted and sliced
- 3 cups hot cooked couscous

Choucroute Garni

This melange (pronounced "shoo-kroot gar-nee") of sauerkraut and meats seasoned with white wine and juniper berries hails from the Alsatian region of France.

Prep: 15 minutes **Cook:** 10 hours on low or 4½ hours on high **Makes:** 4 servings

---

2 small cooking apples

2 fully cooked knackwurst

2 medium potatoes, quartered

2 medium carrots, cut into
  ½-inch pieces (1 cup)

½ cup chopped onion

3 juniper berries, crushed
  (optional)

1 bay leaf

2 medium smoked pork loin
  chops, cut ¾ inch thick
  (about 12 ounces),
  or 8 ounces fully cooked
  ham slice, cut into pieces

1 1-pound can sauerkraut,
  drained

½ cup water

½ cup dry white wine

1 teaspoon instant chicken
  bouillon granules

⅛ teaspoon ground cloves

⅛ teaspoon ground black
  pepper

1. Core apples and cut into quarters. Score knackwurst diagonally. In a 3½- or 4-quart slow cooker place potatoes, carrots, onion, juniper berries, (if desired) bay leaf, pork chops, sauerkraut, apples, and knackwurst. Combine water, wine, bouillon granules, cloves, and pepper; add to cooker.

2. Cover; cook on low-heat setting for 10 to 12 hours or on high heat setting for 4½ to 5 hours. Discard bay leaf.

For 5- or 6-quart slow cooker: Use 3 cooking apples, 3 fully cooked knackwurst, 3 potatoes, quartered, 3 carrots, cut into ½-inch pieces, ¾ cup chopped onion, 5 juniper berries, crushed (optional), 2 bay leaves, 3 medium smoked pork loin chops, cut ¾ inch thick, or 12 ounces fully cooked ham slice, cut into pieces, one 27-ounce can sauerkraut, drained, ¾ cup water, ¾ cup dry white wine, 1½ teaspoons instant chicken bouillon granules, ⅛ teaspoon ground cloves, and ¼ teaspoon ground black pepper. Prepare as above. Makes 6 servings.

Nutrition Facts per serving: 361 calories, 17 g total fat, 46 mg cholesterol, 1,745 mg sodium, 34 g carbohydrate, 16 g protein.

Smoked Sausage and Beans

Top each serving of this four-bean and sausage dish with sour cream or plain yogurt.

Prep: 10 minutes **Cook:** 8 hours on low or 4 hours on high **Makes:** 8 servings

1. In a 3½-, 4-, or 5-quart slow cooker combine kidney beans, black beans, Great Northern beans, butter beans, sausage, ketchup, sweet pepper, onion, brown sugar, garlic, Worcestershire sauce, mustard, and hot pepper sauce. Stir all ingredients together.

2. Cover; cook on low-heat setting for 8 to 10 hours or on high-heat setting for 4 to 5 hours.

Nutrition Facts per serving: 372 calories, 8 g total fat, 30 mg cholesterol, 1,499 mg sodium, 58 g carbohydrate, 24 g protein.

1 15½-ounce can
   red kidney beans, undrained
1 15-ounce can black beans,
   rinsed and drained
1 15-ounce can Great Northern
   beans, rinsed and drained
1 15-ounce can butter beans,
   rinsed and drained
1 pound fully cooked smoked
   turkey sausage, halved
   lengthwise and cut into
   ½-inch slices
1½ cups ketchup
1 medium green sweet pepper,
   chopped (¾ cup)
½ cup chopped onion
¼ cup packed brown sugar
2 cloves garlic, minced
1 teaspoon Worcestershire
   sauce
½ teaspoon dry mustard
½ teaspoon bottled hot
   pepper sauce

Italian-Sausage Heros

These state-fair favorites can easily be made at home. Enjoy them with cold lemonade.

Prep: 20 minutes **Cook:** 10 hours on low **Makes:** 8 servings

1 pound bulk Italian sausage

½ pound ground beef

1 cup chopped onion

1 15-ounce can tomato sauce

1 7½-ounce can tomatoes, undrained and cut up

1 4-ounce can mushroom stems and pieces, drained

½ cup sliced pitted ripe olives

4 teaspoons quick-cooking tapioca

1 teaspoon sugar

1 teaspoon dried oregano, crushed

⅛ teaspoon ground black pepper

Dash garlic powder

8 French-style rolls, split lengthwise

6 ounces sliced mozzarella cheese

1. In a large skillet cook sausage, ground beef, and onion until meat is brown and onion is tender. Drain off fat.

2. Meanwhile, in a 3½- or 4-quart slow cooker combine tomato sauce, tomatoes, mushrooms, olives, tapioca, sugar, oregano, pepper, and garlic powder. Stir in meat mixture. Cover; cook on low-heat setting for 10 to 12 hours.

3. Using a fork, hollow out bottom halves of rolls, leaving ¼-inch-thick shells. (Reserve bread pieces for another use.) Place cheese in bottom halves, trimming as necessary to fit. Spoon meat mixture into rolls. Cut remaining cheese into strips and place on top of meat mixture. Cover with bun tops.

For 5- or 6-quart slow cooker: Double all ingredients; prepare as above. Makes 16 servings.

Nutrition Facts per serving: 425 calories, 22 g total fat, 68 mg cholesterol, 1,073 mg sodium, 29 g carbohydrate, 23 g protein.

Chorizo Sausage Sandwiches

Chorizo is a spicy Mexican sausage seasoned with lots of garlic and chili powder. If you can't find it at your local supermarket, you'll no doubt find it an Hispanic food market.

Prep: 25 minutes **Cook:** 8 hours on low or 4 hours on high **Makes:** 16 servings

1. Remove casing from chorizo (if using). In a large skillet cook sausage and ground turkey, half at a time, until meat is cooked through. Drain off fat. In a 5- or 6-quart slow cooker combine onion, tomato sauce, tomatoes, tapioca, jalapeño peppers, sugar, and oregano. Stir in the meat.

2. Cover; cook on low-heat setting for 8 to 10 hours or on high-heat setting for 4 to 5 hours. Using a fork, hollow out bottom halves of rolls, leaving a ¼-inch-thick shell. Spoon meat mixture into roll bottoms. Add roll tops. If desired, serve with sliced olives, shredded cheese, and/or cherry peppers.

Nutrition Facts per serving: 253 calories, 8 g total fat, 21 mg cholesterol, 593 mg sodium, 35 g carbohydrate, 14 g protein.

- 1 **pound chorizo sausage or bulk Italian sausage**
- 2 **pounds ground raw turkey or lean ground beef**
- 2 **cups chopped onion**
- 1 **15-ounce can tomato sauce**
- 1 **14½-ounce can diced tomatoes, undrained**
- 2 **tablespoons quick-cooking tapioca**
- 2 **tablespoons finely chopped, seeded jalapeño peppers**
- 2 **teaspoons sugar**
- 2 **teaspoons dried oregano, crushed**
- 16 **French-style rolls, split lengthwise**
   Sliced pitted ripe olives (optional)
   Shredded Monterey jack cheese (optional)
   Mild sliced cherry peppers (optional)

Fettuccine with Sausage and Mushrooms

Earthy cremini mushrooms are immature portobello mushrooms. They impart a woodsy flavor to this pasta sauce. Button mushrooms would be a fine substitute.

Prep: 15 minutes **Cook:** 6 hours on low or 3 hours on high **Makes:** 6 to 8 servings

12 ounces bulk sweet
    Italian sausage
2 cups sliced fresh cremini
    and/or button mushrooms
1 28-ounce can
    crushed tomatoes,
    undrained
1 8-ounce can tomato sauce
1 6-ounce can tomato paste
⅔ cup water
1 medium onion, chopped
1 tablespoon sugar
1 teaspoon dried rosemary,
    crushed, or 1 tablespoon
    snipped fresh rosemary
¼ teaspoon ground black
    pepper
2 cloves garlic, minced
9 to 12 ounces dried
    fettuccine, spaghetti,
    or mafalda
    Freshly shredded or grated
    Parmesan cheese
    (optional)

1. In a large skillet brown sausage. Drain off fat. In a 3½- or 4-quart slow cooker combine mushrooms, tomatoes, tomato sauce, tomato paste, water, onion, sugar, rosemary, pepper, and garlic. Stir in sausage.

2. Cover; cook on low-heat setting for 6 to 8 hours or on high-heat setting for 3 to 4 hours.

3. Just before serving, cook pasta according to package directions; drain. Serve sausage mixture over pasta. If desired, sprinkle with Parmesan cheese.

Nutrition Facts per serving: 358 calories, 10 g total fat, 22 mg cholesterol, 938 mg sodium, 54 g carbohydrate, 14 g protein.

Curried Lamb and Rice

Serve this classic curried lamb with a salad of fresh spinach, cucumber, and tomato.

Prep: 20 minutes **Cook:** 7 hours on low or 3½ hours on high **Stand:** 5 minutes **Makes:** 6 servings

1. Trim fat from lamb roast. In a large skillet brown roast on all sides in hot oil.

2. Meanwhile, in a 3½- or 4-quart slow cooker combine vegetable juice, rice, curry powder, and salt. Add carrots. Place meat on carrots.

3. Cover; cook on low-heat setting for 7 to 8 hours or on high-heat setting for 3½ to 4 hours.

4. Add the sweet pepper to the slow cooker. Cover and let stand 5 to 10 minutes.

Nutrition Facts per serving: 367 calories, 13 g total fat, 89 mg cholesterol, 544 mg sodium, 32 g carbohydrate, 29 g protein.

1 2- to 2½-pound boneless
   lamb shoulder roast
1 tablespoon cooking oil
2½ cups hot-style
   vegetable juice
1 cup uncooked brown rice
1 teaspoon curry powder
¼ teaspoon salt
2 medium carrots,
   cut into ½-inch pieces
   (1 cup)
1 medium green sweet pepper,
   cut into ½-inch strips
   (¾ cup)

Honey-Spiced Lamb and Vegetables

An unusual combination of spices—ginger, anise, cinnamon, and red pepper—gives this lamb roast an exotic richness. Serve it with hot cooked couscous and tender sweet beans (cooked green soybeans).

Prep: 25 minutes **Cook:** 10 hours on low or 5 hours on high **Makes:** 6 to 8 servings

1 2½- to 3-pound boneless lamb shoulder roast
1 tablespoon cooking oil
1½ pounds whole tiny new potatoes or 5 medium potatoes
2 cups whole tiny carrots
2 small onions, cut into wedges
1¼ cups beef broth
1 tablespoon honey
1 tablespoon grated fresh ginger or ¾ teaspoon ground ginger
½ teaspoon salt
½ teaspoon anise seeds or ¼ teaspoon ground allspice
½ teaspoon ground cinnamon
⅛ to ¼ teaspoon ground red pepper
½ cup cold water
¼ cup all-purpose flour
1½ teaspoons finely shredded orange peel

1. Trim the fat from the lamb roast. If necessary, cut roast to fit into a 3½-, 4-, or 5-quart slow cooker. In a large skillet brown roast on all sides in hot oil.

2. Meanwhile, remove a narrow strip of peel from the center of each new potato, or peel (if desired) and quarter each medium potato.

3. In slow cooker place potatoes, carrots, and onions. Place meat on vegetables. In a bowl combine beef broth, honey, ginger, salt, anise seeds, cinnamon, and red pepper. Pour over meat and vegetables.

4. Cover; cook on low-heat setting for 10 to 12 hours or on high-heat setting for 5 to 6 hours.

5. Remove meat and vegetables with slotted spoon; keep warm. For gravy, skim fat from juices; measure 1½ cups juices. In a saucepan, combine cold water, flour, and orange peel. Stir in the reserved 1½ cups of juices. Cook and stir until thickened and bubbly. Cook and stir 1 minute more. If desired, season to taste. Pass gravy with the meat and vegetables.

Nutrition Facts per serving: 462 calories, 17 g total fat, 111 mg cholesterol, 468 mg sodium, 41 g carbohydrate, 37 g protein.

Mustard-Sauced Lamb and Artichokes

The best way to make finely shredded lemon peel is to use a small tool called a citrus zester to create long strips of peel, then use a pair of clean kitchen shears to snip the strips into small shreds.

Prep: 30 minutes **Cook:** 10 hours on low plus 30 minutes on high or 4½ hours on high **Makes:** 4 servings

1. Trim fat from lamb roast. If necessary, cut roast to fit into a 3½- or 4-quart slow cooker. In a small bowl combine lemon-pepper seasoning and dry mustard. Sprinkle evenly over sides of lamb roast; rub lightly with fingers. In a large skillet brown the roast on all sides in hot oil.

2. Meanwhile, in the slow cooker place potatoes and carrots. Place meat on top of vegetables. In a bowl combine broth, mustard, tapioca, lemon juice, rosemary, lemon peel, pepper, and garlic; pour over all in slow cooker.

3. Cover; cook on low-heat setting for 10 to 12 hours or on high-heat setting for 4 to 5 hours.

4. If using low-heat setting, turn to high-heat setting. Add artichoke hearts. Cover and cook 30 minutes longer on high-heat setting. Skim fat from gravy and serve with roast.

Nutrition Facts per serving: **590 calories, 21 g total fat, 133 mg cholesterol, 824 mg sodium, 52 g carbohydrate, 47 g protein.**

1 2- to 2½-pound boneless lamb shoulder roast
½ teaspoon lemon-pepper seasoning
½ teaspoon dry mustard
1 tablespoon cooking oil
4 medium potatoes, quartered
1½ cups whole tiny carrots
1 cup chicken broth
3 tablespoons Dijon-style mustard
2 tablespoons quick-cooking tapioca
1 tablespoon lemon juice
½ teaspoon dried rosemary, crushed
¼ teaspoon finely shredded lemon peel
¼ teaspoon ground black pepper
2 cloves garlic, minced
1 9-ounce package frozen artichoke hearts, thawed

Moroccan-Style Lamb

Fill your kitchen with the exotic aromas of a North African spice market. Substitute raisins or golden raisins for the currants, if you like.

Prep: 15 minutes **Cook:** 9 hours on low plus 5 minutes on high or 4 hours and 35 minutes on high **Makes:** 8 servings

2 pounds lean boneless lamb, fat removed, cut into 1-inch pieces

2 large carrots, peeled and cut into 1-inch pieces

2 large onions, peeled and quartered

2 cups chicken broth

3 medium tomatoes, chopped

1½ teaspoons ground cumin

¼ teaspoon crushed red pepper (optional)

1 teaspoon ground turmeric

1 10-ounce package quick-cooking couscous (1½ cups)

¼ cup currants

1. In a 3½- or 4-quart slow cooker combine lamb, carrots, onions, broth, tomatoes, cumin, pepper, and ½ teaspoon of the turmeric.

2. Cover; cook on low-heat setting for 9 to 10 hours or on high-heat setting for 4½ to 5½ hours.

3. Transfer lamb mixture to a serving bowl using a slotted spoon, leaving juices in cooker. If using low-heat setting, turn to high-heat setting. Stir in remaining ½ teaspoon turmeric, couscous, and currants. Cover; cook for 5 to 7 minutes. Fluff couscous with a fork. Divide couscous among eight pasta dishes. Spoon lamb mixture over couscous.

Nutrition Facts per serving: **330 calories, 5 g total fat, 73 mg cholesterol, 339 mg sodium, 39 g carbohydrate, 30 g protein.**

Winter Night Osso Buco

The squash and Brussels sprouts are poetic license—additions to this traditional Italian dish. Serve it as the Italians do—with saffron risotto—and a garnish of minced parsley, lemon peel, and garlic.

Prep: 25 minutes **Cook:** 8 hours on low plus 45 minutes on high or 4 hours 45 minutes on high **Makes:** 4 servings

1. In a 10-inch skillet brown veal shanks or beef ribs, half at a time, in hot oil. Transfer the meat to a 3½- to 4-quart slow cooker, reserving drippings in skillet. Sprinkle the meat with pepper.

2. Add onion and garlic to skillet. Add more oil if necessary. Reduce heat to medium; cook until onion is tender, stirring occasionally. Add chicken broth, scraping bottom of the pan to loosen any browned bits.

3. Transfer the onion mixture with juices to the slow cooker. Add potatoes. Cover; cook on the low-heat setting for 8 to 9 hours or on high-heat setting for 4 to 4½ hours or until meat is nearly tender.

4. Add squash, Brussels sprouts, and horseradish to cooker, rearranging so vegetables are in cooking liquid. Stir together cornstarch and water; stir into mixture in cooker. If using low heat setting, turn to high heat setting. Cook, covered, for 45 to 60 minutes or until vegetables are just tender. Transfer meat and vegetables to a serving platter. If desired, sprinkle with parsley.

Nutrition Facts per serving: 474 calories, 14 g total fat, 139 mg cholesterol, 626 mg sodium, 42 g carbohydrate, 46 g protein.

4 veal shank cross cuts
  (2 pounds) or 1½ pounds
  boneless beef short ribs
2 tablespoons olive oil
¼ teaspoon ground black
  pepper
1 large onion, chopped
3 cloves garlic, minced
1 10½-ounce can condensed
  chicken broth
8 new potatoes, halved
1½ cups cubed, peeled butternut
  squash (1- to 1½-inch
  cubes) (about 1 pound
  unpeeled)
1 10-ounce package frozen
  Brussels sprouts
1 tablespoon prepared
  horseradish
2 tablespoons cornstarch
2 tablespoons cold water
  Snipped fresh parsley
  (optional)

poultry

A chicken in every pot is an attractive proposition,
especially when it happens to be a slow cooker that
can turn any bird (turkey too!) into succulent eating.

Chicken with Creamy Chive Sauce, page 180

Barbecue-Style Chicken

Too cold to fire up the grill and you have a craving for some all-American barbecued chicken?
Fire up the slow cooker instead.

Prep: 25 minutes **Cook:** 10 hours on low or 5 hours on high **Makes:** 4 to 5 servings

2 medium unpeeled potatoes,
  cut into ½-inch pieces
1 large green sweet pepper,
  cut into strips
1 medium onion, sliced
1 tablespoon quick-cooking
  tapioca
2 pounds chicken thighs
  or drumsticks, skin
  and fat removed
1 8-ounce can tomato sauce
2 tablespoons packed
  brown sugar
1 tablespoon Worchestershire
  sauce
1 tablespoon yellow mustard
1 clove garlic, minced
¼ teaspoon salt

1. In a 3½- to 4-quart slow cooker place potatoes, sweet pepper, and onion. Sprinkle tapioca over vegetables. Place chicken pieces on top.

2. In a small bowl stir together tomato sauce, brown sugar, Worchestershire sauce, mustard, garlic, and salt. Pour mixture over chicken in slow cooker. Cover; cook on low-heat setting for 10 to 12 hours or on high-heat setting for 5 to 6 hours. To serve, transfer the chicken and vegetables to a serving bowl. Skim fat from the sauce, then pour sauce over chicken and vegetables.

Nutrition Facts per serving: 282 calories, 5 g total fat, 107 mg cholesterol, 670 mg sodium, 30 g carbohydrate, 29 g protein.

Cashew-Ginger Chicken

Serve this Chinese-style dish with oolong tea and fortune cookies or almond cookies for dessert.

Prep: 15 minutes **Cook:** 6 hours on low or 3 hours on high **Makes:** 6 servings

1. In a 3½- or 4-quart slow cooker stir together the soup, soy sauce, and ginger until combined. Stir in the chicken tenders, celery, carrot, water chestnuts, and mushrooms.

2. Cover; cook on low-heat setting for 6 to 8 hours or on high-heat setting for 3 to 4 hours. Stir cashews into chicken mixture. Serve over hot cooked rice.

Nutrition Facts per serving: 368 calories, 9 g total fat, 68 mg cholesterol, 789 mg sodium, 38 g carbohydrate, 33 g protein.

1 10¾-ounce can condensed golden mushroom soup
2 tablespoons soy sauce
½ teaspoon ground ginger
1½ pounds chicken tenders
1 cup sliced celery
1 cup purchased shredded carrot
1 8-ounce can sliced water chestnuts, drained
1 cup sliced fresh mushrooms or one 4-ounce can sliced mushrooms, drained
½ cup cashews
3 cups hot cooked rice

Chicken à la Roma

Artichokes and olives give tender chicken pieces an Italian accent. Serve them with hot cooked linguine and sprinkle a little fresh-grated Romano cheese on top, if you like.

Prep: 15 minutes **Cook:** 7 hours on low or 3½ hours on high **Makes:** 4 to 6 servings

2 cups sliced fresh
   mushrooms
1 14½-ounce can tomato
   wedges, drained
1 9-ounce package frozen
   artichoke hearts
½ cup sliced, pitted ripe olives
3 tablespoons quick-cooking
   tapioca
2 to 2½ pounds chicken
   breasts, thighs,
   and/or legs, skinned
¾ cup chicken broth
¼ cup dry white wine
   or chicken broth
1 tablespoon dried Italian
   seasoning, crushed
4 ounces linguine, cooked
   and drained

1. In a 3½- or 4-quart slow cooker combine the mushrooms, tomato wedges, artichoke hearts, and olives. Sprinkle with tapioca. Place the chicken pieces on top of the vegetables.

2. In a bowl combine the chicken broth, white wine, and Italian seasoning. Pour over the chicken.

3. Cover; cook on low-heat setting for 7 to 8 hours or on high-heat setting for 3½ to 4 hours. Serve with hot cooked linguine.

Nutrition Facts per serving: 397 calories, 10 g total fat, 81 mg cholesterol, 538 mg sodium, 42 g carbohydrate, 35 g protein.

Chicken and Dumplings

Sometimes nothing but comfort food will do. Old-fashioned stewed chicken topped with fluffy cheddar-cheese dumplings is a sure cure for anything that ails you.

Prep: 25 minutes **Cook:** 8 hours on low plus 25 minutes on high or 4 hours and 25 minutes on high **Makes:** 8 servings

1. In a 4- or 5-quart slow cooker place carrots, potatoes, parsnips, garlic, bay leaves, sage, ½ teaspoon of the salt, and of the pepper. Top with chicken pieces. In a medium bowl gradually whisk broth into soup. Pour broth mixture over chicken and vegetables.

2. Cover; cook on low-heat setting for 8 to 10 hours or on high-heat setting for 4 to 5 hours.

3. If using low-heat setting, turn to high heat setting. In a medium bowl combine flour, cheddar cheese, cornmeal, baking powder, and the remaining ¼ teaspoon salt. Combine egg, milk, and melted butter and stir into flour mixture until just combined. Stir stew and remove bay leaves from stew. Combine water and cornstarch; stir into stew. Drop dumplings by tablespoonfuls on top of stew.

4. Cover; cook for 25 to 30 minutes more or until toothpick inserted into dumplings comes out clean.

Nutrition Facts per serving: 361 calories, 14 g total fat, 140 mg cholesterol, 948 mg sodium, 29 g carbohydrate, 29 g protein.

- 2 cups chopped carrots
- 2 cups chopped potatoes, peeled if desired
- 1½ cups chopped parsnips
- 1 clove garlic, minced
- 2 bay leaves
- 1 teaspoon dried sage, crushed
- ¾ teaspoon salt
- ¼ teaspoon ground black pepper
- 2 pounds boneless, skinless chicken thighs, cut in 1-inch pieces
- 1 14-ounce can chicken broth
- 1 10¾-ounce can condensed cream of chicken soup
- ½ cup all-purpose flour
- ½ cup shredded cheddar cheese
- ⅓ cup yellow cornmeal
- 1 teaspoon baking powder
- 1 egg, beaten
- 2 tablespoons milk
- 2 tablespoons butter, melted
- 2 tablespoons water
- 1 tablespoon cornstarch

Chicken and Mushrooms

You can certainly use just one kind of mushroom for this earthy chicken dish, but a variety will give it more interesting texture and flavor.

Prep: 25 minutes **Cook:** 7 hours on low or 3½ hours on high **Makes:** 6 servings

5 cups sliced, assorted fresh
    mushrooms, such as
    shiitake, button, crimini,
    and oyster
1 medium onion, chopped
½ cup chopped carrot
¼ cup dried tomato pieces
    (not oil-packed)
¾ cup chicken broth
¼ cup dry white wine
    or chicken broth
3 tablespoons quick-cooking
    tapioca
1 teaspoon dried thyme,
    crushed
½ teaspoon dried basil,
    crushed
½ teaspoon garlic salt
¼ to ½ teaspoon ground black
    pepper
3 pounds chicken thighs
    or drumsticks (with bone),
    skinned
4½ cups hot cooked plain
    and/or spinach linguine
    or fettuccine,
    or hot cooked rice

1. In a 4- or 5-quart slow cooker combine mushrooms, onion, carrot, and tomato pieces. Pour chicken broth and wine over all. Sprinkle with tapioca, thyme, basil, garlic salt, and pepper. Place chicken pieces on top of vegetables.

2. Cover; cook on low-heat setting for 7 to 8 hours or on high-heat setting for 3½ to 4 hours. To serve, arrange chicken and vegetables over pasta or rice; spoon juices on top.

Nutrition Facts per serving: 360 calories, 7 g total fat, 107 mg cholesterol, 350 mg sodium, 39 g carbohydrate, 34 g protein.

Chicken and Shrimp Jambalaya

If you like your Cajun food spicy, use the Homemade Cajun Seasoning blend. Our three-pepper combo packs more wallop than the supermarket variety.

Prep: 20 minutes **Cook:** 5 hours on low or 2½ hours on high **Stand:** 10 minutes **Makes:** 6 servings

1. In a 3½- or 4-quart slow cooker combine celery, onion, tomatoes, broth, tomato paste, Worcestershire sauce, and Cajun seasoning. Stir in chicken.

2. Cover; cook on low-heat setting for 5 to 6 hours or on high-heat setting for 2½ to 3 hours. Stir in rice, shrimp, and sweet pepper. Cover and let stand 10 to 15 minutes or until most of the liquid is absorbed and rice is tender.

Homemade Cajun Seasoning: In a small bowl combine ¼ teaspoon white pepper, ¼ teaspoon garlic powder, ¼ teaspoon onion powder, ⅛ to ¼ teaspoon ground red pepper, ¼ teaspoon paprika, and ¼ teaspoon ground black pepper.

Nutrition Facts per serving: 261 calories, 2 g total fat, 118 mg cholesterol, 391 mg sodium, 30 g carbohydrate, 30 g protein.

1 cup sliced celery

1 large onion, chopped (1 cup)

1 14½-ounce can reduced-sodium tomatoes, undrained and cut-up

1 14-ounce can reduced-sodium chicken broth

½ of a 6-ounce can tomato paste (⅓ cup)

1 tablespoon Worcestershire sauce

1½ teaspoons Cajun seasoning or 1 recipe Homemade Cajun Seasoning

1 pound skinless, boneless chicken breast halves or thighs, cut into ¾-inch pieces

1½ cups instant rice

8 ounces cooked peeled, deveined shrimp

¾ cup chopped green sweet pepper

Chicken Cacciatore

Cacciatora is Italian for hunter. The Italian-American word "cacciatore" refers to anything served "hunter-style"—with onions, mushrooms, tomatoes, and herbs.

Prep: 25 minutes **Cook:** 6 hours on low plus 15 minutes on high or 3¼ hours on high **Makes:** 6 servings

---

  2 cups sliced fresh
     mushrooms
  1 cup sliced celery
  1 cup chopped carrot
  2 medium onions, cut into
     wedges
  1 green, yellow, or red sweet
     pepper, cut into strips
  4 cloves garlic, minced
 12 chicken drumsticks, skinned
     (about 3½ pounds)
  ½ cup chicken broth
  ¼ cup dry white wine
  2 tablespoons quick-cooking
     tapioca
  2 bay leaves
  1 teaspoon dried oregano,
     crushed
  1 teaspoon sugar
  ½ teaspoon salt
  ¼ teaspoon ground black
     pepper
  1 14½-ounce can diced
     tomatoes, undrained
  ⅓ cup tomato paste
     Hot cooked pasta or rice

1. In a 5- or 6-quart slow cooker combine mushrooms, celery, carrot, onions, sweet pepper, and garlic. Place chicken on top of vegetables. Combine broth, wine, tapioca, bay leaves, oregano, sugar, salt, and pepper; pour over chicken.

2. Cover; cook on low-heat setting for 6 to 7 hours or on high-heat setting for 3 to 3½ hours.

3. Remove chicken and keep warm. Remove bay leaves and discard. If using low-heat setting, turn to high-heat setting. Stir in undrained tomatoes and tomato paste. Cover; cook 15 minutes longer on high-heat setting. Spoon vegetable mixture over chicken and pasta to serve.

Nutrition Facts per serving: 365 calories, 6 g total fat, 114 mg cholesterol, 507 mg sodium, 37 g carbohydrate, 38 g protein.

Chicken and Shrimp with Orzo

This elegant dish is ideal for entertaining, served with a salad of baby greens and a light white wine, such as a Sauvignon Blanc. Finish the meal sweetly with a fresh fruit tart and coffee.

Prep: 15 minutes **Cook:** 6 hours on low plus 5 minutes on high or 3 hours and 5 minutes on high **Makes:** 4 to 5 servings

---

1. Cut chicken thighs into quarters. In a 3½-, 4-, or 5-quart slow cooker place the onion and garlic. Top with the chicken pieces. In a bowl combine the tomatoes, tomato paste, wine, lemon juice, bay leaves, salt, and red pepper. Pour over all.

2. Cover; cook on low-heat setting for 6 to 7 hours or on high-heat setting for 3 to 3½ hours.

3. If using low-heat setting, turn to high-heat setting. Remove bay leaves. Stir in shrimp and artichoke hearts. Cover; cook for 5 minutes more. Serve chicken and shrimp mixture over hot cooked orzo. Sprinkle with feta cheese.

Nutrition Facts per serving: 615 calories, 21 g total fat, 187 mg cholesterol, 1,203 mg sodium, 56 g carbohydrate, 46 g protein.

12 ounces skinless, boneless
    chicken thighs
1 large onion, chopped
3 cloves garlic, minced
1 14½-ounce can diced
    tomatoes with basil, garlic,
    and oregano, or diced
    tomatoes with onion
    and garlic, undrained
2 tablespoons tomato paste
½ cup port wine
    or chicken broth
2 tablespoons lemon juice
2 bay leaves
½ teaspoon salt
¼ teaspoon crushed red pepper
1 8-ounce package frozen
    peeled, cooked shrimp,
    thawed and drained
1 9-ounce package frozen
    artichoke hearts, thawed
    and coarsely chopped
2 cups hot cooked orzo
    (rosamarina)
½ cup crumbled feta cheese
    (2 ounces)

Chicken Curry

If you're just getting acquainted with Indian-style cooking, this classic dish is a terrific place to start. Curry powder ranges from mild to hot; read the label to discern the heat level of the bottle you buy.

Prep: 30 minutes **Cook:** 6 hours on low plus 30 minutes on high or 3½ hours on high **Makes:** 8 servings

---

  3 tablespoons all-purpose flour
  3 tablespoons curry powder
1½ teaspoons ground cumin
  1 teaspoon salt
1½ pounds boneless, skinless
      chicken breasts or thighs,
      cut in 1-inch pieces
  2 cups peeled and
      chopped potatoes
1½ cups bias-sliced carrots
  1 cup coarsely chopped
      cooking apple
¾ cup chopped onion
  2 cloves garlic, minced
  1 jalapeño pepper, seeded
      and finely chopped
  1 teaspoon instant chicken
      bouillon granules
½ cup water
  1 13½-ounce can
      unsweetened coconut milk
      Hot cooked rice
      Raisins
      Chopped peanuts

1. In a large resealable plastic bag place flour, curry powder, cumin, and salt. Add chicken pieces; seal and shake to coat.

2. In a 3½- or 4-quart slow cooker place potatoes, carrots, apple, onion, garlic, jalapeño, and chicken bouillon. Top with chicken pieces. Pour water over chicken.

3. Cover; cook on low-heat setting for 6 to 8 hours or on high-heat setting for 3 to 4 hours.

4. If using low-heat setting, turn to high-heat setting. Stir in coconut milk; cover and cook on high-heat setting 30 minutes more. Serve over cooked rice and top with raisins and chopped peanuts.

Nutrition Facts per serving: 409 calories, 14 g total fat, 49 mg cholesterol, 513 mg sodium, 45 g carbohydrate, 26 g protein.

Chicken Mole

Mexican cooking encompasses far more than burritos and tacos. The complex flavors of this mole (pronounced MO-lay) made with chiles and chocolate pair beautifully with the mild taste of chicken.

Prep: 15 minutes **Cook:** 9 hours on low or 4½ hours on high **Makes:** 6 servings

---

1. For mole sauce, in a blender container or food processor bowl combine tomatoes, chicken broth, onion, ¼ cup almonds, jalapeño peppers, cocoa powder, raisins, sesame seeds, garlic, sugar, cinnamon, nutmeg, and coriander. Cover and blend or process to a coarse puree.

2. In a 3½-, 4-, 5-, or 6-quart slow cooker place tapioca. Add chicken; then sauce. Cover; cook on low-heat setting for 9 to 11 hours or on high-heat setting for 4½ to 5½ hours.

3. Arrange chicken over rice on a platter. Skim fat from sauce; pour sauce over chicken. Sprinkle with 2 tablespoons almonds.

Nutrition Facts per serving: 448 calories, 23 g total fat, 99 mg cholesterol, 586 mg sodium, 24 g carbohydrate, 36 g protein.

1 7½-ounce can tomatoes, undrained
¾ cup chicken broth
½ cup chopped onion
¼ cup slivered almonds
1 to 2 canned jalapeño peppers, drained
3 tablespoons unsweetened cocoa powder
3 tablespoons raisins
1 tablespoon sesame seeds
3 cloves garlic
1 teaspoon sugar
¼ teaspoon ground cinnamon
⅛ teaspoon ground nutmeg
⅛ teaspoon ground coriander
2 tablespoons quick-cooking tapioca
1 2½- to 3-pound broiler-fryer chicken, cut up and skinned
Hot cooked rice
2 tablespoons slivered almonds, toasted

Chicken Merlot with Mushrooms

Although it's called Chicken Merlot, you can use any dry red wine—such as a Cabernet Sauvignon, Syrah, or Burgundy—to make this wine-and-mushroom chicken dish.

Prep: 25 minutes **Cook:** 7 hours on low or 3½ hours on high **Makes:** 4 to 6 servings

3 cups sliced fresh
    mushrooms
1 large onion, chopped
2 cloves garlic, minced
2½ to 3 pounds meaty chicken
    pieces (breasts, thighs,
    and drumsticks), skinned
¾ cup chicken broth
1 6-ounce can tomato paste
¼ cup dry red wine (such as
    Merlot) or chicken broth
2 tablespoons quick-cooking
    tapioca
2 tablespoons snipped fresh
    basil or 1½ teaspoons
    dried basil, crushed
2 teaspoons sugar
¼ teaspoon salt
¼ teaspoon ground black
    pepper
2 cups hot cooked noodles
2 tablespoons finely shredded
    Parmesan cheese

1. In a 3½-, 4-, or 5-quart slow cooker place mushrooms, onion, and garlic. Place chicken pieces on top of the vegetables. In a bowl combine broth, tomato paste, wine, tapioca, dried basil (if using), sugar, salt, and pepper. Pour over all.

2. Cover; cook on low-heat setting for 7 to 8 hours or on high-heat setting for 3½ to 4 hours. If using, stir in fresh basil. To serve, spoon chicken, mushroom mixture, and sauce over hot cooked noodles. Sprinkle with Parmesan cheese.

Nutrition Facts per serving: 469 calories, 12 g total fat, 144 mg cholesterol, 468 mg sodium, 41 g carbohydrate, 46 g protein.

Chicken Spaghetti Sauce

Everybody loves spaghetti with tomato sauce! Try this version made with ground turkey or chicken. To make it extra-lean, look for white-meat-only ground poultry that is ground without the skin.

Prep: 25 minutes **Cook:** 8 hours on low or 4 hours on high **Makes:** 8 to 10 servings

---

1. Brown meat with garlic in a large skillet until no longer pink. Drain fat.

2. In a 3½- or 4-quart slow cooker place meat mixture, tomatoes, tomato paste, pepper, Italian seasoning, salt, bay leaf, and, if desired, hot pepper sauce.

3. Cover; cook on low-heat setting for 8 to 9 hours or on high-heat setting for 4 to 4½ hours. Remove bay leaf and discard. Serve sauce over pasta. If desired, sprinkle with grated Parmesan cheese.

Nutrition Facts per serving: 379 calories, 6 g total fat, 45 mg cholesterol, 540 mg sodium, 60 g carbohydrate, 21 g protein.

1 pound ground raw turkey
  or chicken
6 cloves garlic, minced
3 14½-ounce cans
  stewed tomatoes, undrained
2 6-ounce cans tomato paste
½ cup chopped green
  sweet pepper
1½ teaspoons dried Italian
  seasoning, crushed
½ teaspoon salt
1 bay leaf
⅛ teaspoon bottled
  hot pepper sauce (optional)
  Hot cooked pasta
  Grated Parmesan cheese
  (optional)

Chicken with Creamy Chive Sauce

Delicate strands of angel hair pasta cloaked in a creamy mushroom and onion sauce make this chicken dish just heavenly. It's also terrific served over hot cooked rice.

Prep: 15 minutes **Cook:** 4 hours on low **Makes:** 6 servings

6 skinless, boneless
   chicken breast halves
   (about 1½ pounds)
¼ cup butter
1 0.7-ounce package dry
   Italian salad dressing mix
1 10¾-ounce can condensed
   golden mushroom soup
½ cup dry white wine
½ of an 8-ounce tub cream
   cheese with chives
   and onion
   Hot cooked angel hair pasta
   Snipped fresh chives
   (optional)

1. Place chicken in a 3½- or 4-quart slow cooker. In a medium saucepan melt the butter. Stir in the dry dressing mix. Stir in mushroom soup, white wine, and cream cheese until combined. Pour over the chicken. Cover and cook on low-heat setting for 4 to 5 hours.

2. Serve chicken and sauce over hot cooked pasta. If desired, sprinkle with chives.

Nutrition Facts per serving: 405 calories, 17 g total fat, 110 mg cholesterol, 1,043 mg sodium, 26 g carbohydrate, 32 g protein.

Chicken with Vegetables and Stuffing

Here's chicken and stuffing the easy way—and it's a great use for leftover chicken or turkey.

Prep: 25 minutes **Cook:** 5 hours on low or 2½ hours on high **Makes:** 6 servings

1. Prepare stuffing mix according to package instructions, except reduce water to ½ cup. (Stuffing will not be completely moistened.) Set aside.

2. In a large bowl combine chicken, zucchini, mushrooms, sweet pepper, and onion. Stir in soup.

3. In a 3½-, 4-, or 5-quart slow cooker place half of the chicken-vegetable mixture; top with half of the stuffing. Repeat.

4. Cover; cook on low-heat setting for 5 to 6 hours or on high-heat setting for 2½ to 3 hours.

Nutrition Facts per serving: 315 calories, 11 g total fat, 52 mg cholesterol, 976 mg sodium, 29 g carbohydrate, 24 g protein.

1 6-ounce package chicken
   flavor stuffing mix
2½ cups chopped cooked
   chicken
2 cups zucchini, cut into
   ½-inch pieces
2 cups sliced fresh mushrooms
1 medium red or green
   sweet pepper, cut into
   ½-inch pieces
½ cup chopped onion
1 10¾-ounce can condensed
   cream of chicken soup or
   cream of mushroom soup

Cranberry Lemon Chicken

A kiss of honey gives this citrus and cranberry chicken just a touch of sweetness.

Prep: 15 minutes **Cook:** 6 hours on low or 3 hours on high **Makes:** 6 servings

1 medium onion, thinly sliced

2 medium apples, cored and
   cut into wedges

1 16-ounce can whole
   cranberry sauce

¼ cup frozen lemonade
   concentrate, thawed

2 tablespoons quick-cooking
   tapioca

2 tablespoons honey

¼ teaspoon salt

6 skinless, boneless
   chicken breast halves
   (about 2 pounds)

2 6-ounce packages long
   grain and wild rice mix

1. In a 3½- or 4-quart slow cooker layer onion and apples. In a medium bowl stir together cranberry sauce, lemonade concentrate, tapioca, honey, and salt. Add chicken breasts, one at a time, to cranberry mixture, turning to coat. Place chicken breasts on top of apples. Pour cranberry mixture over chicken breasts.

2. Cover; cook on low-heat setting for 6 to 7 hours or on high-heat setting for 3 to 3½ hours.

3. Meanwhile, prepare long grain and wild rice according to package directions. Serve chicken and sauce over rice.

Nutrition Facts per serving: 565 calories, 2 g total fat, 88 mg cholesterol, 993 mg sodium, 96 g carbohydrate, 40 g protein.

Creamy Chicken and Noodles

Long-cooking chicken and noodles isn't just for Sunday dinner anymore. The slow cooker version of this family favorite can be enjoyed any day of the week.

Prep: 25 minutes **Cook:** 8 hours on low or 4 hours on high **Makes:** 6 servings

---

1. In a 3½- or 4-quart slow cooker place carrots, onion, celery, parsley, and bay leaf. Place chicken on top of vegetables. In a bowl stir together soup, water, thyme, and pepper. Pour over chicken and vegetables.

2. Cover; cook on low-heat setting for 8 to 9 hours or on high-heat setting for 4 to 4½ hours. Remove chicken from cooker; cool slightly. Remove and discard bay leaf.

3. Meanwhile, cook noodles according to package directions; drain. Stir peas into soup mixture in cooker. Remove chicken from bones; discard bones. Cut meat into bite-size pieces; stir into cooker. To serve, pour chicken mixture over noodles; toss gently to combine. If desired, season to taste with salt and pepper.

Nutrition Facts per serving: 406 calories, 7 g total fat, 122 mg cholesterol, 532 mg sodium, 56 g carbohydrate, 28 g protein.

- 2 cups sliced carrots
- 1½ cups chopped onion
- 1 cup sliced celery
- 2 tablespoons snipped fresh parsley
- 1 bay leaf
- 3 medium chicken legs (drumstick-thigh portion), skinned (about 2 pounds)
- 2 10¾-ounce cans reduced-fat and reduced-sodium condensed cream of chicken soup
- ½ cup water
- 1 teaspoon dried thyme, crushed
- ¼ teaspoon ground black pepper
- 10 ounces dried wide noodles (about 5 cups)
- 1 cup frozen peas
- Salt (optional)
- Pepper (optional)

Garlic Chicken with Artichokes

A dozen cloves of garlic may sound like overload, but the garlic mellows and sweetens as it cooks, enveloping the chicken in aroma and flavor.

Prep: 20 minutes **Cook:** 6 hours on low or 3 hours on high **Makes:** 6 servings

12 cloves garlic, minced

1 medium onion, chopped

1 tablespoon olive oil
   or cooking oil

1 8- or 9-ounce package
   frozen artichoke hearts

1 red sweet pepper,
   cut into strips

½ cup chicken broth

1 tablespoon quick-cooking
   tapioca

2 teaspoons dried rosemary,
   crushed

1 teaspoon finely shredded
   lemon peel

½ teaspoon ground
   black pepper

1½ pounds skinless, boneless
   chicken breast halves
   or thighs

4 cups hot cooked brown rice

1. In a small skillet cook garlic and onion in hot oil over medium heat, stirring occasionally, 5 minutes or until tender. In a 3½- or 4-quart slow cooker combine the frozen artichoke hearts, garlic mixture, sweet pepper, chicken broth, tapioca, rosemary, lemon peel, and black pepper. Add chicken; spoon some of the garlic mixture over chicken.

2. Cover; cook on low-heat setting for 6 to 7 hours or on high-heat setting for 3 to 3½ hours. Serve with rice.

Nutrition Facts per serving: **341 calories, 6 g total fat, 66 mg cholesterol, 159 mg sodium, 39 g carbohydrate, 32 g protein.**

One-Pot Winter Dinner

You don't have to cook the onion in the bacon drippings, but the bacon does add a delicious smoky flavor to this homey dish. Even with the bacon, it still has only 4 grams of fat per serving.

Prep: 15 minutes **Cook:** 7 hours on low or 3½ hours on high **Makes:** 6 to 8 servings

1. In a skillet cook chicken, bacon, and onion until chicken is no longer pink. Drain off fat. Transfer mixture to a 3½- or 4-quart slow cooker. Gently stir in the pork and beans, butter and kidney beans, ketchup, brown sugar, vinegar, Liquid Smoke, salt, and pepper.

2. Cover; cook on low-heat setting for 7 to 8 hours or on high-heat setting for 3½ to 4 hours.

Nutrition Facts per serving: 395 calories, 4 g total fat, 28 mg cholesterol, 1,685 mg sodium, 76 g carbohydrate, 25 g protein.

½ pound ground raw chicken

5 slices bacon, cut up,
  or 2 tablespoons cooking oil

1 cup chopped onion

2 31-ounce cans pork and
  beans in tomato sauce

1 15½-ounce can butter
  beans, rinsed and drained

1 15-ounce can dark red kidney
  beans, rinsed and drained

1 cup ketchup

¼ cup packed brown sugar

3 tablespoons vinegar

1 teaspoon Liquid Smoke

  Dash salt

  Dash ground black pepper

Greek Chicken and Orzo

For the most authentic Greek flavor, use kalamata olives, which have a rich, salty, fruity flavor and grow in abundance all over the Greek islands.

Prep: 25 minutes **Cook:** 5 hours on low or 2½ hours on high **Makes:** 4 servings

4 medium chicken
    breast halves (about
    1½ pounds total)
2 tablespoons cooking oil
1 medium fennel bulb, cut into
    ½-inch pieces (2 cups)
1 medium onion,
    cut into wedges
2 cloves garlic, minced
2 cups water
2 tablespoons white
    balsamic vinegar
2 teaspoons instant chicken
    bouillon granules
1 tablespoon snipped fresh
    oregano or 1 teaspoon
    dried oregano, crushed
¼ teaspoon crushed
    red pepper
1⅓ cups dried orzo pasta
    (rosamarina)
1 medium tomato, chopped
¼ cup crumbled feta cheese
    (1 ounce)
¼ cup chopped pitted
    ripe olives
1 tablespoon snipped
    fresh oregano

1. Skin chicken. In a large skillet brown chicken breasts in hot oil. In a 3½- or 4-quart slow cooker combine fennel, onion, and garlic. Add the chicken breasts. In a bowl stir together water, balsamic vinegar, bouillon granules, dried oregano (if using), and red pepper. Pour over all.

2. Cover; cook on low-heat setting for 5 to 6 hours or on high-heat setting for 2½ to 3 hours. If using, stir in the 1 tablespoon fresh oregano.

3. Cook the orzo according to package directions; drain. Stir tomato, cheese, olives, and the 1 tablespoon fresh oregano into orzo. Using a slotted spoon, remove chicken and vegetables from cooker. Serve with orzo mixture.

Nutrition Facts per serving: 439 calories, 12 g total fat, 58 mg cholesterol, 626 mg sodium, 53 g carbohydrate, 28 g protein.

Italian Chicken and Green Beans

Italian-style green beans are broad and thick and make for toothsome eating. You can also use regular cut green beans with no change in the flavor of this Italian-style dish.

Prep: 15 minutes **Cook:** 5 hours on low or 2½ hours on high **Makes:** 4 servings

1. Cut chicken into 1-inch pieces.

2. In a 3½- or 4-quart slow cooker place green beans, mushrooms, and onion. Place chicken on top of vegetables.

3. In a small bowl combine tomatoes, tomato paste, Italian seasoning, and garlic. Pour over chicken.

4. Cover; cook on low-heat setting for 5 to 6 hours or on high-heat setting for 2½ to 3 hours. Serve over hot cooked fettuccine. If desired, pass grated Parmesan cheese.

Nutrition Facts per serving: 308 calories, 4 g total fat, 45 mg cholesterol, 799 mg sodium, 44 g carbohydrate, 24 g protein.

12 ounces skinless, boneless
　　chicken breast halves
1 9-ounce package frozen
　　Itallan-style green beans
1 cup fresh mushrooms,
　　quartered
1 small onion, sliced
　　¼ inch thick
1 14½-ounce can Italian-style
　　stewed tomatoes, undrained
1 6-ounce can Italian-style
　　tomato paste
1 teaspoon dried Italian
　　seasoning, crushed
2 cloves garlic, minced
4 ounces fettuccine,
　　cooked and drained
　　Grated Parmesan cheese
　　(optional)

Herbed Chicken and Vegetables

Use a fairly dry white wine such as a Chardonnay or Sauvignon Blanc to make this light dish of tender, falling-off-the-bone chicken and vegetables in an aromatic herbed wine sauce.

Prep: 25 minutes **Cook:** 8 hours on low or 4 hours on high **Makes:** 6 servings

---

3 pounds chicken legs, thighs, or drumsticks, skinned

2 tablespoons cooking oil

1 cup chicken broth

½ cup dry white wine

1 tablespoon snipped fresh parsley

½ teaspoon salt

½ teaspoon dried rosemary, crushed

½ teaspoon dried thyme, crushed

¼ teaspoon ground black pepper

1 clove garlic, minced

4 medium potatoes, quartered

4 medium carrots, cut into ½-inch pieces

2 stalks celery, cut into 1-inch pieces

1 small onion, sliced

2 tablespoons cornstarch

2 tablespoons cold water

1. In a skillet brown chicken pieces, half at a time, in hot oil.

2. In a bowl combine the chicken broth, wine, parsley, salt, rosemary, thyme, pepper, and garlic.

3. In a 3½-, 4-, or 5-quart slow cooker place potatoes, carrots, celery, and onion. Place chicken pieces on top of vegetables. Pour broth mixture over chicken.

4. Cover; cook on low-heat setting for 8 to 9 hours or on high-heat setting for 4 to 4½ hours.

5. Using a slotted spoon, remove chicken and vegetables to a platter. Keep chicken and vegetables warm.

6. For gravy, skim fat from cooking juices. Strain juices into a saucepan. Combine cornstarch and cold water; stir into juices in saucepan. Cook and stir until thickened and bubbly. Cook and stir 2 minutes more. Pass the gravy with the chicken and vegetables.

Nutrition Facts per serving: 338 calories, 10 g total fat, 79 mg cholesterol, 416 mg sodium, 31 g carbohydrate, 27 g protein.

Orange Teriyaki Chicken

Garnish each serving of this sweet and fruity chicken with fresh orange slices and toasted almonds.

Prep: 15 minutes **Cook:** 4 hours on low or 2 hours on high **Makes:** 4 servings

1. Cut chicken into 1-inch pieces.

2. In a 3½-, 4-, or 5-quart slow cooker place vegetables. Sprinkle tapioca over vegetables. Place chicken pieces on top of vegetables.

3. For sauce, in a small bowl combine chicken broth, brown sugar, teriyaki sauce, mustard, orange peel, and ginger. Pour sauce over chicken pieces.

4. Cover; cook on low-heat setting for 4 to 6 hours or on high-heat setting for 2 to 3 hours. Serve with hot cooked rice.

Nutrition Facts per serving: 303 calories, 4 g total fat, 60 mg cholesterol, 543 mg sodium, 39 g carbohydrate, 27 g protein.

1 pound skinless, boneless
  chicken breast halves
  or thighs
1 16-ounce package loose-pack
  frozen broccoli,
  baby carrots, and
  water chestnuts
2 tablespoons quick-cooking
  tapioca
½ cup chicken broth
2 tablespoons packed brown
  sugar
2 tablespoons teriyaki sauce
1 teaspoon dry mustard
1 teaspoon finely shredded
  orange peel
½ teaspoon ground ginger
2 cups hot cooked rice

Southwest Barbecue-Style Chicken

Sweet and hot jalapeño pepper jelly is the secret ingredient in this delicious barbecued chicken. Serve it with black beans, avocado slices, and warmed flour tortillas.

Prep: 10 minutes **Cook:** 6 hours on low or 3 hours on high **Makes:** 4 to 6 servings

½ cup tomato sauce

2 tablespoons jalapeño
   pepper jelly

2 tablespoons lime
   or lemon juice

2 tablespoons quick-cooking
   tapioca

1 teaspoon packed brown
   sugar

1 teaspoon ground cumin

¼ to ½ teaspoon crushed
   red pepper

2 to 2½ pounds chicken
   breasts, thighs,
   and/or legs, skinned

1. In a 3½- or 4-quart slow cooker combine tomato sauce, jelly, lime juice, tapioca, brown sugar, cumin, and red pepper. Place chicken on top of sauce mixture, meaty side down.

2. Cover; cook on low-heat setting for 6 to 7 hours or on high-heat setting for 3 to 3½ hours.

Nutrition Facts per serving: 227 calories, 7 g total fat, 81 mg cholesterol, 264 mg sodium, 15 g carbohydrate, 26 g protein.

Spicy Ginger and Tomato Chicken

Simple but sophisticated, this super-light dish gets its great flavor from a just-right balance of tomato, ginger, garlic, crushed red pepper—and a touch of brown sugar for sweetness.

Prep: 15 minutes **Cook:** 6 hours on low or 3 hours on high **Makes:** 6 servings

1. Place chicken pieces in a 3½- or 4-quart slow cooker.

2. Drain 1 can of tomatoes; chop tomatoes from both cans. For sauce, in a medium bowl combine both cans of tomatoes, tapioca, ginger, cilantro, garlic, brown sugar, red pepper, and salt. Pour sauce over chicken.

3. Cover; cook on low-heat setting for 6 to 7 hours or on high-heat setting for 3 to 3½ hours. Skim fat from sauce. Serve sauce with chicken and couscous or rice.

Nutrition Facts per serving: 332 calories, 11 g total fat, 66 mg cholesterol, 507 mg sodium, 33 g carbohydrate, 25 g protein.

1 2½- to 3-pound cut up boiler-fryer chicken, skinned

2 16-ounce cans tomatoes

2 tablespoons quick-cooking tapioca

1 tablespoon grated ginger

1 tablespoon snipped fresh cilantro or parsley

4 cloves garlic, minced

2 teaspoons packed brown sugar

½ to 1 teaspoon crushed red pepper

½ teaspoon salt

3 cups hot cooked couscous or rice

Sweet and Tangy Spiced Chicken

A homemade citrus barbecue sauce made with the juices of lemon, pineapple, and orange—and spiced with cinnamon, allspice, and cloves—gives this easy chicken dish a pleasant tang.

Prep: 20 minutes **Cook:** 8 hours on low or 4 hours on high **Makes:** 6 servings

1 6-ounce can frozen
    pineapple-orange juice
    concentrate, thawed
½ cup ketchup
2 tablespoons lemon juice
2 tablespoons quick-cooking
    tapioca
2 inches stick cinnamon,
    broken
8 whole allspice
4 whole cloves
2½ to 3 pounds meaty
    chicken pieces
    (breast halves, thighs,
    and drumsticks) skinned
Hot cooked couscous

1. For sauce, in a small bowl combine juice concentrate, ketchup, and lemon juice. Pour about half of the sauce into a 3½- or 4-quart slow cooker. Add tapioca to the cooker; stir. For spice bag, place cinnamon, allspice, and cloves in cheesecloth and tie. Add bag to cooker. Place chicken pieces in slow cooker. Pour remaining sauce over chicken.

2. Cover; cook on low-heat setting for 8 hours or on high-heat setting for 4 hours. Discard spice bag. Transfer chicken to a serving platter. Skim fat from sauce. Serve sauce and hot couscous with chicken.

For 5- or 6-quart slow cooker: Double all ingredients. Prepare as above. Makes 12 servings.

Nutrition Facts per serving: **471 calories, 9 g total fat, 115 mg cholesterol, 479 mg sodium, 54 g carbohydrate, 41 g protein.**

Thyme and Garlic Chicken Breasts

A few simple ingredients—garlic, thyme, orange juice, and a splash of balsamic vinegar—result in a big flavor payoff for these chicken breasts. Serve them with a package of saffron rice and steamed peas.

Prep: 15 minutes **Cook:** 5 hours on low or 2½ hours on high **Boil:** 10 minutes **Makes:** 6 to 8 servings

1. Sprinkle garlic and thyme over chicken. Place chicken pieces in a 3½- or 4-quart slow cooker. Pour orange juice and vinegar over chicken.

2. Cover and cook on low-heat setting for 5 to 6 hours or on high-heat setting for 2½ to 3 hours.

3. Remove chicken from cooker; cover and keep warm. Skim off fat from cooking juices. Strain juices into a saucepan. Bring to boiling; reduce heat. Boil gently, uncovered, for 10 minutes or until reduced to 1 cup. Pass juices to spoon over chicken.

Nutrition Facts per serving: **178 calories, 2 g total fat, 85 mg cholesterol, 78 mg sodium, 3 g carbohydrate, 34 g protein.**

- **6 cloves garlic, minced**
- **1½ teaspoons dried thyme, crushed**
- **3 to 4 pounds whole chicken breasts (with bone), halved and skinned**
- **¼ cup orange juice**
- **1 tablespoon balsamic vinegar**

Rosemary Chicken with Pasta

As this aromatic meal finishes cooking, make a spinach salad with baby spinach, blue cheese crumbles, croutons, Italian dressing—and lots of coarsely ground black pepper.

Prep: 10 minutes **Cook:** 7 hours on low or 3½ hours on high **Makes:** 4 servings

2 medium onions, sliced or chopped

2 teaspoons bottled minced garlic or 4 cloves garlic, minced

12 ounces skinless, boneless chicken breasts or thighs

1 14½-ounce can diced tomatoes, undrained

1 6-ounce can tomato paste

2 tablespoons wine vinegar

2 bay leaves

1 teaspoon sugar

½ teaspoon dried rosemary, crushed

¼ teaspoon salt

¼ teaspoon ground black pepper

1 4-ounce can sliced mushrooms, drained

8 ounces dried pasta (such as penne, mostaccioli, or elbow macaroni)

Grated Parmesan cheese

1. In a 3½-, 4-, or 4½-quart slow cooker place the onions and garlic. Add chicken to cooker.

2. In a bowl combine tomatoes, tomato paste, vinegar, bay leaves, sugar, rosemary, salt, and pepper; mix well. Pour over chicken.

3. Cover; cook on low-heat setting for 7 hours or on high-heat setting for 3½ hours.

4. When ready to serve, remove bay leaves. Stir mushrooms into chicken mixture; cook for 5 to 10 minutes more to heat through. Meanwhile, cook pasta according to package directions. Serve the chicken and sauce over the hot cooked pasta; sprinkle with Parmesan cheese.

Nutrition Facts per serving: 415 calories, 5 g total fat, 47 mg cholesterol, 568 mg sodium, 65 g carbohydrate, 29 g protein.

Weeknight Chicken and Rice

After a long day at work, school, or errand-running, having this satisfying chicken and rice dish ready and waiting is a simple pleasure.

Prep: 15 minutes **Cook:** 5 hours on low plus 10 minutes on high or 2 hours and 40 minutes on high **Makes:** 4 servings

1. In a 3½- or 4-quart slow cooker combine mushrooms, celery, onion, dill, and pepper. Place chicken on top of vegetables. Combine soup and broth and pour over chicken mixture.

2. Cover; cook on low-heat setting for 5 to 6 hours or on high-heat setting for 2½ to 3 hours. Stir in rice. If using low heat setting, turn to high; cover and cook for 10 more minutes.

Nutrition Facts per serving: **516 calories, 12 g total fat, 108 mg cholesterol, 840 mg sodium, 66 g carbohydrate, 34 g protein.**

- **2 cups sliced fresh mushrooms**
- **1 cup sliced celery**
- **½ cup chopped onion**
- **1½ teaspoons dried dill**
- **¼ teaspoon ground black pepper**
- **2 pounds chicken thighs, skinned**
- **1 10¾-ounce can condensed cream of mushroom or cream of chicken soup**
- **¾ cup chicken broth**
- **1½ cups instant rice**

Barbecue-Style Turkey Thighs

Add an extra pinch of crushed red pepper if you like your barbecue on the spicy side.

Prep: 10 minutes **Cook:** 10 hours on low or 5 hours on high **Makes:** 4 to 6 servings

½ cup ketchup

2 tablespoons packed brown sugar

1 tablespoon quick-cooking tapioca

1 tablespoon vinegar

1 teaspoon Worcestershire sauce

¼ teaspoon ground cinnamon

¼ teaspoon crushed red pepper

2 to 2½ pounds turkey thighs (about 2 thighs) or meaty chicken pieces (breasts, thighs, and drumsticks), skinned

Hot cooked rice or noodles (optional)

1. In a 3½ or 4-quart slow cooker combine ketchup, brown sugar, tapioca, vinegar, Worcestershire sauce, cinnamon, and red pepper. Place turkey thighs on top of ketchup mixture, meaty side down and flat in the cooker.

2. Cover; cook on low-heat setting for 10 to 12 hours or high-heat setting for 5 to 6 hours. If desired, serve turkey and sauce over rice or noodles.

For 5- or 6-quart slow cooker: Use ¾ cup ketchup, 3 tablespoons brown sugar, 4 teaspoons quick-cooking tapioca, 4 teaspoons vinegar, 2 teaspoons Worcestershire sauce, ¼ teaspoon ground cinnamon, ¼ teaspoon red pepper, and 3 to 3½ pounds turkey thighs, skinned. Prepare as above. Makes 6 to 8 servings.

Nutrition Facts per serving: 239 calories, 6 g total fat, 100 mg cholesterol, 449 mg sodium, 16 g carbohydrate, 30 g protein.

Fruited Turkey in Red Wine Sauce

Turkey thighs get dressed up with a savory compote of dried apricots, prunes, red wine, garlic, thyme, and honey. Serve it with hot cooked rice or couscous.

Prep: 30 minutes **Cook:** 6 hours on low or 3 hours on high **Makes:** 4 or 5 servings

1. Remove skin from turkey thighs. In a large skillet brown turkey in hot oil. Transfer turkey to a 3½- or 4-quart slow cooker. Place prunes and apricots on top of turkey.

2. Stir together orange juice, wine, garlic, honey, lemon peel, thyme, and salt. Pour orange juice mixture over turkey.

3. Cover; cook on low-heat setting for 6 to 7 hours or on high-heat setting for 3 to 3½ hours.

4. Using a slotted spoon, transfer turkey and fruit to a serving platter; cover turkey and keep warm. Pour cooking juices into a glass measure; skim off fat. For sauce, measure 1¼ cups juices. Transfer to a saucepan. Combine the cornstarch and cold water; stir into juices in saucepan. Cook and stir over medium heat until thickened and bubbly. Cook and stir for 2 minutes more. Spoon sauce over turkey and hot cooked rice.

Nutrition Facts per serving: **531 calories, 14 g total fat, 156 mg cholesterol, 406 mg sodium, 49 g carbohydrate, 47 g protein.**

3 pounds turkey thighs
1 tablespoon cooking oil
½ cup pitted prunes
½ cup dried apricot halves
½ cup orange juice
¼ cup dry red wine
4 cloves garlic, minced
1 tablespoon honey
1 tablespoon finely shredded
   lemon peel
2 teaspoons dried thyme,
   crushed
½ teaspoon salt
1 tablespoon cornstarch
1 tablespoon cold water
   Hot cooked rice

Maple-Mustard Turkey Thighs

Round out this yummy anytime meal with mashed potatoes (stir in some bottled minced and roasted garlic for flavor) and steamed green beans.

Prep: 10 minutes **Cook:** 6 hours on low or 2½ hours on high **Makes:** 6 servings

2 to 2½ pounds turkey thighs (about 2 thighs), skinned
½ cup maple syrup or maple-flavored syrup
⅓ cup coarse-grain brown mustard
1 tablespoon quick-cooking tapioca

1. Place turkey thighs in the bottom of a 3½- or 4-quart slow cooker.

2. In a small bowl stir together syrup, mustard, and tapioca. Pour over turkey.

3. Cover; cook on low-heat setting for 6 to 7 hours or on high-heat setting for 2½ to 3 hours.

Nutrition Facts per serving: 263 calories, 8 g total fat, 81 mg cholesterol, 255 mg sodium, 19 g carbohydrate, 28 g protein.

Turkey Roast Chablis

Here's the perfect dish for a small holiday gathering when a whole bird is just too much.

Serve it with a crisp green salad topped with toasted pecans and dried cranberries.

Prep: 20 minutes **Cook:** 10 hours on low or 4½ hours on high **Makes:** 6 to 8 servings

1. In a 3½-, 4-, 5-, or 6-quart slow cooker combine white wine, onion, garlic, and bay leaf. If turkey roast is wrapped in netting, remove and discard. If gravy packet is included, remove packet from roast; refrigerate packet for another use. Combine rosemary and pepper. Rub roast with rosemary mixture. Place turkey roast in cooker.

2. Cover; cook on low-heat setting for 10 to 12 hours or on high-heat setting for 4½ to 5½ hours. Remove roast and keep warm. For gravy, strain cooking juices; discard solids. Skim fat from juices. Measure 1⅓ cups juices into a small saucepan. Combine cream, cornstarch, and salt; stir into juices. Cook and stir until thickened and bubbly. Cook and stir 2 minutes more.

3. Slice turkey roast. Spoon some gravy over roast. Pass remaining gravy with roast.

Nutrition Facts per serving: 324 calories, 6 g total fat, 125 mg cholesterol, 1,594 mg sodium, 19 g carbohydrate, 41 g protein.

¾ cup dry white wine
½ cup chopped onion
1 clove garlic, minced
1 bay leaf
1 3 to 3½-pound frozen boneless turkey roast, thawed
1 teaspoon dried rosemary, crushed
¼ teaspoon ground black pepper
⅓ cup light cream or milk
2 tablespoons cornstarch
⅛ teaspoon salt

Turkey Meatballs and Gravy

Using a package of gravy mix as a starter for a savory herbed gravy makes this family-pleasing dinner doable any day of the week.

Prep: 30 minutes **Cook:** 6 hours on low or 3 hours on high **Makes:** 8 servings

2 eggs, beaten

¾ cup fine dry seasoned bread crumbs

½ cup finely chopped onion

½ cup finely chopped celery

2 tablespoons snipped fresh parsley

¼ teaspoon ground black pepper

⅛ teaspoon garlic powder

2 pounds ground raw turkey

1½ teaspoons cooking oil

1 10¾-ounce can reduced-sodium condensed cream of mushroom soup

1 cup water

1 15⁄16-ounce envelope turkey gravy mix

½ teaspoon finely shredded lemon peel

½ teaspoon dried thyme, crushed

1 bay leaf

Hot cooked mashed potatoes or buttered noodles

Snipped fresh parsley (optional)

1. In a large bowl combine eggs, bread crumbs, onion, celery, 2 tablespoons parsley, pepper, and garlic powder. Add ground turkey and mix well. Shape into 1½-inch balls.

2. In a large skillet brown meatballs, half at a time, in hot oil. If necessary add additional oil. Drain meatballs. Transfer to a 3½- or 4-quart slow cooker.

3. In a bowl combine soup, water, gravy mix, lemon peel, thyme, and bay leaf. Pour over meatballs.

4. Cover; cook on low-heat setting for 6 to 8 hours or on high-heat setting for 3 to 4 hours. Discard bay leaf. Serve with mashed potatoes or noodles. If desired, sprinkle with additional snipped fresh parsley.

Nutrition Facts per serving: 314 calories, 14 g total fat, 98 mg cholesterol, 916 mg sodium, 25 g carbohydrate, 21 g protein.

Chicken and Rice Burritos

You're no longer limited to plain flour or corn tortillas. Exercise your flatbread options and wrap this zippy chicken and rice filling in green spinach or orange chile flour tortillas.

Prep: 25 minutes **Cook:** 6 hours on low or 3 hours on high **Stand:** 5 minutes **Makes:** 6 to 8 servings

1. Cut zucchini in half lengthwise and then into ¾-inch slices. In a 3½- or 4-quart slow cooker combine zucchini, sweet pepper, onion, and celery. Top with chicken strips. In a small bowl combine taco sauce, bouillon granules, and cumin. Pour over chicken.

2. Cover; cook on low-heat setting for 6 to 7 hours or on high-heat setting for 3 to 3½ hours. Stir in rice. Cover and let stand for 5 minutes.

3. Warm tortillas according to package directions. Divide chicken mixture evenly among warmed tortillas. Top with shredded cheese, tomato, and green onion. Fold bottom edge of each tortilla up and over filling. Fold opposite sides in, just until they meet. Roll up from bottom. Secure with wooden toothpicks, if necessary.

Nutrition Facts per serving: 408 calories, 10 g total fat, 81 mg cholesterol, 735 mg sodium, 43 g carbohydrate, 35 g protein.

- 1 medium zucchini
- 1 large green sweet pepper, cubed
- 1 medium onion, coarsely chopped
- ½ cup coarsely chopped celery
- 1½ pounds skinless, boneless chicken breast halves, cut into ½-inch strips
- 1 8-ounce bottle green taco sauce
- 1 teaspoon instant chicken bouillon granules
- ½ teaspoon ground cumin
- 1 cup instant rice
- 6 to 8 nine- to ten-inch spinach, chile, or plain flour tortillas
- ¾ cup shredded Monterey Jack cheese with jalapeño peppers (3 ounces)
- 2 small tomatoes, chopped
- 2 green onions, sliced

Sweet-and-Sour Chicken with Almonds

Five ingredients add up to a terrific Chinese-style dinner.

Prep: 10 minutes **Cook:** 5 hours on low or 2½ hours on high **Makes:** 4 servings

---

1 pound skinless, boneless chicken breast halves

1 24½-ounce jar sweet-and-sour cooking sauce for chicken

1 16-ounce package loose-pack frozen broccoli, carrots, water chestnuts, and red sweet peppers

2 cup hot cooked rice

¼ cup toasted, chopped almonds

1. Cut chicken into 1-inch pieces.

2. In a 3½- or 4-quart slow cooker combine chicken, sweet-and-sour sauce, and vegetables.

3. Cover; cook on low-heat setting for 5 to 6 hours or on high-heat setting for 2½ to 3 hours. Serve with hot cooked rice. Sprinkle with almonds.

Nutrition Facts per serving: 415 calories, 7 g total fat, 59 mg cholesterol, 526 mg sodium, 62 g carbohydrate, 27 g protein.

Index

Metric Information

The charts on this page provide a guide for converting measurements from the U.S. customary system, which is used throughout this book, to the metric system.

Product Differences

Most of the ingredients called for in the recipes in this book are available in most countries. However, some are known by different names. Here are some common American ingredients and their possible counterparts:

- Sugar (white) is granulated, fine granulated, or castor sugar.
- Powdered sugar is icing sugar.
- All-purpose flour is enriched, bleached or unbleached, white household flour. When self-rising flour is used in place of all-purpose flour in a recipe that calls for leavening, omit the leavening agent (baking soda or baking powder) and salt.
- Light-colored corn syrup is golden syrup.
- Cornstarch is cornflour.
- Baking soda is bicarbonate of soda.
- Vanilla or vanilla extract is vanilla essence.
- Green, red, or yellow sweet peppers are capsicums or bell peppers.
- Golden raisins are sultanas.

Volume and Weight

The United States traditionally uses cup measures for liquid and solid ingredients. The chart below shows the approximate imperial and metric equivalents. If you are accustomed to weighing solid ingredients, the following approximate equivalents will be helpful.

- 1 cup butter, castor sugar, or rice = 8 ounces = ½ pound = 250 grams
- 1 cup flour = 4 ounces = ¼ pound = 125 grams
- 1 cup icing sugar = 5 ounces = 150 grams

Canadian and U.S. volume for a cup measure is 8 fluid ounces (237 ml), but the standard metric equivalent is 250 ml.

1 British imperial cup is 10 fluid ounces.

In Australia, 1 tablespoon equals 20 ml, and there are 4 teaspoons in the Australian tablespoon.

Spoon measures are used for smaller amounts of ingredients. Although the size of the tablespoon varies slightly in different countries, for practical purposes and for recipes in this book, a straight substitution is all that's necessary. Measurements made using cups or spoons always should be level unless stated otherwise.

Common Weight Range Replacements

Imperial / U.S.	Metric
½ ounce	15 g
1 ounce	25 g or 30 g
4 ounces (¼ pound)	115 g or 125 g
8 ounces (½ pound)	225 g or 250 g
16 ounces (1 pound)	450 g or 500 g
1¼ pounds	625 g
1½ pounds	750 g
2 pounds or 2¼ pounds	1,000 g or 1 Kg

Oven Temperature Equivalents

Fahrenheit Setting	Celsius Setting*	Gas Setting
300°F	150°C	Gas Mark 2 (very low)
325°F	160°C	Gas Mark 3 (low)
350°F	180°C	Gas Mark 4 (moderate)
375°F	190°C	Gas Mark 5 (moderate)
400°F	200°C	Gas Mark 6 (hot)
425°F	220°C	Gas Mark 7 (hot)
450°F	230°C	Gas Mark 8 (very hot)
475°F	240°C	Gas Mark 9 (very hot)
500°F	260°C	Gas Mark 10 (extremely hot)
Broil	Broil	Grill

*Electric and gas ovens may be calibrated using celsius. However, for an electric oven, increase celsius setting 10 to 20 degrees when cooking above 160°C. For convection or forced air ovens (gas or electric), lower the temperature setting 25°F/10°C when cooking at all heat levels.

Baking Pan Sizes

Imperial / U.S.	Metric
9×1½-inch round cake pan	22- or 23×4-cm (1.5 L)
9×1½-inch pie plate	22- or 23×4-cm (1 L)
8×8×2-inch square cake pan	20×5-cm (2 L)
9×9×2-inch square cake pan	22- or 23×4.5-cm (2.5 L)
11×7×1½-inch baking pan	28×17×4-cm (2 L)
2-quart rectangular baking pan	30×19×4.5-cm (3 L)
13×9×2-inch baking pan	34×22×4.5-cm (3.5 L)
15×10×1-inch jelly roll pan	40×25×2-cm
9×5×3-inch loaf pan	23×13×8-cm (2 L)
2-quart casserole	2 L

U.S./Standard Metric Equivalents

⅛ teaspoon = 0.5 ml	
¼ teaspoon = 1 ml	
½ teaspoon = 2 ml	
1 teaspoon = 5 ml	
1 tablespoon = 15 ml	
2 tablespoons = 25 ml	
¼ cup = 2 fluid ounces = 50 ml	
⅓ cup = 3 fluid ounces = 75 ml	
½ cup = 4 fluid ounces = 125 ml	
⅔ cup = 5 fluid ounces = 150 ml	
¾ cup = 6 fluid ounces = 175 ml	
1 cup = 8 fluid ounces = 250 ml	
2 cups = 1 pint = 500 ml	
1 quart = 1 litre	